EARLY CHILDHOOD EDUCATION SERIES
Sharon Ryan, Editor

ADVISORY BOARD: Barbara T. Bowman, Harriet K. Cuffaro, Stephanie Feeney, Doris Pronin Fromberg, Celia Genishi, Stacie G. Goffin, Dominic F. Gullo, Alice Sterling Honig, Elizabeth Jones, Gwen Morgan

(continued)

The Power of Projects: Meeting Contemporary
Challenges in Early Childhood Classrooms–
Strategies and Solutions
JUDY HARRIS HELM & SALLEE BENEKE, EDS.

Bringing Learning to Life: The Reggio Approach to Early
Childhood Education
LOUISE BOYD CADWELL

The Colors of Learning: Integrating the Visual Arts
into the Early Childhood Curriculum
ROSEMARY ALTHOUSE, MARGARET H. JOHNSON, &
SHARON T. MITCHELL

A Matter of Trust: Connecting Teachers and Learners in
the Early Childhood Classroom
CAROLLEE HOWES & SHARON RITCHIE

Widening the Circle: Including Children with
Disabilities in Preschool Programs
SAMUEL L. ODOM, ED.

Children with Special Needs: Lessons for Early
Childhood Professionals
MARJORIE J. KOSTELNIK, ESTHER ETSUKO ONAGA,
BARBARA ROHDE, & ALICE PHIPPS WHIREN

Developing Constructivist Early Childhood Curriculum:
Practical Principles and Activities
RHETA DEVRIES, BETTY ZAN, CAROLYN HILDEBRANDT,
REBECCA EDMIASTON, & CHRISTINA SALES

Outdoor Play: Teaching Strategies with Young Children
JANE PERRY

Embracing Identities in Early Childhood Education:
Diversity and Possibilities
SUSAN GRIESHABER & GAILE S. CANNELLA, EDS.

Bambini: The Italian Approach to Infant/Toddler Care
LELLA GANDINI & CAROLYN POPE EDWARDS, EDS.

Young Investigators: The Project Approach in the
Early Years
JUDY HARRIS HELM & LILIAN G. KATZ

Serious Players in the Primary Classroom: Empowering
Children Through Active Learning Experiences, 2nd Ed.
SELMA WASSERMANN

Telling a Different Story: Teaching and Literacy in an
Urban Preschool
CATHERINE WILSON

Young Children Reinvent Arithmetic: Implications of
Piaget's Theory, 2nd Ed.
CONSTANCE KAMII

Managing Quality in Young Children's Programs:
The Leader's Role
MARY L. CULKIN, ED.

The Early Childhood Curriculum: A Review of Current
Research, 3rd Ed.
CAROL SEEFELDT, ED.

Leadership in Early Childhood: The Pathway to
Professionalism, 2nd Ed.
JILLIAN RODD

Inside a Head Start Center: Developing Policies from Practice
DEBORAH CEGLOWSKI

Bringing Reggio Emilia Home: An Innovative Approach
to Early Childhood Education
LOUISE BOYD CADWELL

Master Players: Learning from Children at Play
GRETCHEN REYNOLDS & ELIZABETH JONES

Understanding Young Children's Behavior
JILLIAN RODD

Understanding Quantitative and Qualitative Research in
Early Childhood Education
WILLIAM L. GOODWIN & LAURA D. GOODWIN

Diversity in the Classroom, 2nd Ed.
FRANCES E. KENDALL

Developmentally Appropriate Practice in "Real Life"
CAROL ANNE WIEN

Experimenting with the World
HARRIET K. CUFFARO

Quality in Family Child Care and Relative Care
SUSAN KONTOS, CAROLLEE HOWES, MARYBETH SHINN,
& ELLEN GALINSKY

Using the Supportive Play Model
MARGARET K. SHERIDAN, GILBERT M. FOLEY,
& SARA H. RADLINSKI

The Full-Day Kindergarten, 2nd Ed.
DORIS PRONIN FROMBERG

Assessment Methods for Infants and Toddlers
DORIS BERGEN

Young Children Continue to Reinvent Arithmetic–3rd
Grade: Implications of Piaget's Theory
CONSTANCE KAMII WITH SALLY JONES LIVINGSTON

Moral Classrooms, Moral Children
RHETA DEVRIES & BETTY ZAN

Diversity and Developmentally Appropriate Practices
BRUCE L. MALLORY & REBECCA S. NEW, EDS.

Changing Teaching, Changing Schools
FRANCES O'CONNELL RUST

Physical Knowledge in Preschool Education
CONSTANCE KAMII & RHETA DEVRIES

Ways of Assessing Children and Curriculum
CELIA GENISHI, ED.

The Play's the Thing
ELIZABETH JONES & GRETCHEN REYNOLDS

Scenes from Day Care
ELIZABETH BALLIETT PLATT

Making Friends in School
PATRICIA G. RAMSEY

The Whole Language Kindergarten
SHIRLEY RAINES & ROBERT CANADY

Multiple Worlds of Child Writers
ANNE HAAS DYSON

The Good Preschool Teacher
WILLIAM AYERS

The Piaget Handbook for Teachers and Parents
ROSEMARY PETERSON & VICTORIA FELTON-COLLINS

Visions of Childhood
JOHN CLEVERLEY & D. C. PHILLIPS

Ideas Influencing Early Childhood Education
EVELYN WEBER

The Joy of Movement in Early Childhood
SANDRA R. CURTIS

Connecting Emergent Curriculum and Standards in the Early Childhood Classroom

STRENGTHENING CONTENT AND TEACHING PRACTICE

Sydney L. Schwartz
Sherry M. Copeland

Teachers College, Columbia University
New York and London

Published by Teachers College Press, 1234 Amsterdam Avenue, New York, NY 10027

Library of Congress Cataloging-in-Publication Data

Schwartz, Sydney L. (Sydney Lisbeth)
     Connecting emergent curriculum and standards in the early childhood classroom : strengthening content and teaching practice / Sydney L. Schwartz, Sherry M. Copeland.
         p. cm. – (Early childhood education series)
     Includes bibliographical references and index.
     ISBN 978-0-8077-5109-1 (pbk. : alk. paper)
     ISBN 978-0-8077-5110-7 (hardcover : alk. paper)
     1. Early childhood education–United States–Evaluation. 2. Early childhood education–Standards–United States. 3. Accreditation (Education)–United States. I. Copeland, Sherry M. II. Title.
     LB1139.25.S393   2010
     372.19–dc22   2010014216

ISBN 978-0-8077-5109-1 (paper)
ISBN 978-0-8077-5110-7 (hardcover)

Printed on acid-free paper
Manufactured in the United States of America

17   16   15   14   13   12   11   10   8   7   6   5   4   3   2   1

As we think of our grandchildren and the other members of the current generation of children—may they be allowed to grow in their knowledge, understandings and skills in a content-rich action-based, emotionally responsive learning environment.

Contents

Preface

The search to find a way to strengthen the content in early childhood classrooms while preserving the action-based learning environment has been a driving force in our early childhood professional careers for a very long time. For one of us, it took shape in the 1960s while participating in Kenneth Wann's study on *Fostering Intellectual Development in Young Children* (Wann, Dorn, & Liddle, 1962). For the other author, the answer to the question "What is the early childhood curriculum?" was not answered satisfactorily with the phrase "Curriculum is what happens" (Dittmann, 1970). About 25 years ago, when we first met at an early childhood conference, we realized that we shared a common concern, yet from two different professional development perspectives—one being that of the college and the other that of the school district. Many subsequent discussions between us and with our early childhood colleagues about this concern brought us closer to an answer.

This project never would have taken hold without the long-term collaboration between the authors who initially began working together as the worlds of the *University* and the *schools* embraced the idea that the education of teachers is a lifelong endeavor. It begins at the University and continues with inservice activities throughout a teacher's career. The collaboration of the authors has been based upon the recognition that there needs to be a continuity between initial teacher preparation, inservice follow-up by the public sector for novice teachers, and support for achieving the expert level that flows from both advanced study at the University and the establishment of the climate for teachers as researchers in the classroom.

Our efforts toward meeting this challenge had two distinct foci. We realized that we needed to become much clearer about the subject-matter content that young children can begin to understand in a developmentally appropriate environment for young children. We also needed to figure out ways to help teachers incorporate this subject-matter content into their classroom programs based on children's interests. For the first focus, we had the advantage of the fact that in the late 1980s and early 1990s major professional organizations such as the National Council for Teachers of Mathematics were developing content lists for the grades. However, attention to early childhood was not adequately included in that effort until much later. Along with this subject-matter movement, the Standards movement kicked into high gear. The limits to the Standards were that they were stated in behavioral terms rather than in key concepts that young children can begin to understand. The second focus, helping teachers bring content into daily program activities in developmentally appropriate ways, required that we help teachers become fluent with the content ideas as well as expanding their role in interaction during interest center periods.

As we wove in and out between trying to clarify the content and better understand how to help teachers expand the teaching role, we consulted with experts in curriculum content at the university level and with experienced teachers in the field. We worked individually and jointly with teachers in both professional development and college settings to transform ideas about curriculum content into practice. The feedback from teachers helped us better understand the task. Our successes in helping teachers become more confident in their knowledge in the subject areas and effective in their instructional strategies to strengthen children's content learning has served as the core content of this book.

We share with the readers our adventures in working with teachers at both the university and professional development level to expand content and strengthen practice in early childhood action-based learning environments. It is our intent to spur more efforts along this path, to create an army of early childhood professionals who can help us successfully roll back the tide of replacing early childhood action-based programs with sedentary direct instruction.

Acknowledgments

In a major initiative like the one we have engaged in, it is almost impossible to identify the many sources of contribution to our own personal and professional development. For both of us, it began with the mentors we have had throughout our careers, most notably our Doctoral advisors, Kenneth Wann and Leslie Williams. We cannot begin to thank the many other colleagues who have made major impacts on the way we think. We have built on the ideas they introduced into our thinking and we are indebted.

The ideas included in this book represent the efforts of a diverse group of educators who took our ideas and ran with them. First and foremost we want to express our deep gratitude to the talented early childhood teachers who have crossed our paths at the university and elsewhere. As we began to develop a notion about the way to address the need to increase content and meet the standards in an action-based learning environment, we discovered that many members of the early childhood community were on the same quest. Through a number of years and many opportunities for dialogue, we uncovered a rich array of examples of ways to contribute to children's content thinking that we believe makes a difference to long-term learning. The professionals who kept coming back to us to continue the dialogue have been vigorous in challenging our thinking as we developed the structure presented in this book for embedding and expanding content and meeting the challenge presented by the *Standards*. This vitality in the professional community fed our work. Without that enthusiasm, the body of ideas we developed could never have been generated. We also thank the educational leaders who shared our vision and supported teachers as they found ways to embed content into early childhood settings that value children's interests.

A very special thanks go to Betsey Brown and Wynne Shilling who critiqued the manuscript in process—we are grateful for their constructive comments and encouragement; and to Great Neck Community School, Hewlett-Woodmere Franklin Early Childhood Center, and Great Community School for contributions of photographs. Also thanks to our friends and families who graciously tolerated our many absences and excuses for not being available on weekends and holidays, know that we appreciate your understanding and we love you.

CHAPTER 1

Our Response to
the Current Challenge

In today's educational setting, the multiple forces working to reshape the preprimary curriculum nationally and locally have relentlessly tried to impose conventional academic demands on prekindergarten and kindergarten programs. The consequence of this has been the diminishment of the historical action-based, child-centered learning environment and its replacement with a skills-based, direct instruction program. In the past 2 decades, national concerns about the academic achievement of our public schoolchildren has led to the generation of curriculum and program standards, not only for the elementary and high school but also for the prekindergarten and kindergarten programs (National Association for the Education of Young Children & National Association of Early Childhood Specialists [NAEYC & NAECS], 2002; National Council for the Social Studies [NCSS], 2004; National Council of Teachers of Mathematics [NCTM], 2000; National Research Council on Teaching and Learning [NRC], 2005).

The creation of standards has resulted in the adoption of tests and assessments geared toward evaluating whether the children have met *the standards*. These assessments have seriously impacted what is taught and how it is taught—that is the scheduling of curriculum activities in prekindergarten and kindergarten classes. The standards movement has advanced the cause for "a push-down curriculum," in which former 1st-grade instruction is moved into many kindergartens, thereby continuing the push-down effect from kindergarten to prekindergarten (Elkind, 1990). In many early childhood settings in this country, the child-centered approach no longer dominates.

If we don't find ways for the multiple forces to engage in dialogue about our common values, we are seriously at risk of seeing an increasing number of programs for 3- to 6-year-olds that will essentially deprive young children of the necessary opportunities to learn in action-based environments along with the adult support they need. Such support is essential to making connections between the world as young children understand it, and the curriculum demands they will meet in the primary grades (Elkind, 1990; Eisner, 1990).

TWO CURRICULUM MODELS,
ONE COMMON ACADEMIC GOAL

The direct instruction, skills-based curriculum model and the action-based, child-centered curriculum model have one major goal in common. Each is dedicated to supporting children as successful students as they proceed through the grades and each has a body of research studies to support the approach (Goffin & Wilson, 2001). The difference lies in the theoretical views of early childhood development and learning that shape the program design.

The Direct Instruction Model

The direct instruction, skills-based approach flows from learning theories that require the use of direct instructional strategies for building children's academic skills and increasing their acquisition of subject matter content. The approach features the transmission of information during periods of direct instruction by the adult, followed by practice of skills in two different formats. One is structured total group practice followed by teacher-defined actions. *Success for All* is a typical program of this type (Slavin et al., 1996). The other is guided practice in small groups using a variety of materials.

The strength of this approach rests on the ease with which the resultant learning can be documented and connected to current lists of *learning standards* in the core academic subjects for early childhood, specifically, literacy and mathematics.

Advocates for the skills-based, direct instruction approach use behavioral performance lists to prescribe a sequence of lessons in a well-defined curriculum package to ensure children's mastery of the subject. This approach facilitates the use of standardized assessments for accountability, thereby documenting that children have learned each of the skills that they have been taught (Becker, Engelmann, & Rhine, 1981; Gersten, Darch, & Gleason, 1988). The perception of the primary limits of this approach is that the documented gains tend to be lost over time and children's interest in learning is not necessarily sustained.

The Action-Based Model

The action-based, child-centered curriculum model flows from theories that define, in general, the developmental attributes of periods of growth in terms of social-emotional, cognitive, and physical development (Hohmann & Weikart, 1995; Kostelnik, Soderman, & Whiren, 2007; Seefeldt & Wasik, 2006; Wortham, 2001). The primary value rests in an instructional design that supports children's social-emotional development and autonomy as learners. This leads to a program that provides a rich resource of materials which are well organized in centers in the classroom, and a generous amount of time in each session for children to pursue their own interests with the materials and peers. At the core of the program is the belief that young children are the best architects of their own learning, which in turn provides the strongest foundation for nurturing lifelong learners. Adult-directed group activities provide new experiences and introduce curriculum content and conventional academic skills for children to use as they pursue their interests.

A primary strength of this approach is that it nurtures children's learning through their own efforts. Through this process they expand their knowledge and better understand the content that has captured their attention. A perceived limit of this approach is the lack of specific data describing what each child has learned in the pursuit of interests. Observational reports accompanied with work samples that serve as documentation to meet accountability purposes are not seen by many as reliable or valid data. This is partly due to the fact that the information that children collect is shaped by their prior knowledge and understandings (Roschelle, 1995; Williams & DeGaetano, 1985). It is in the very nature of the value placed on respecting children's interests and choices that makes it difficult to collect and organize data in order to document a standard set of outcomes for children who are entering the primary program.

Typical programs of this genre are the Creative Curriculum, the Project Approach, and the Reggio Emilia program, which highlight the inclusion of content and skills from all subject areas when developing an action-based unit, theme, or project (Dodge & Colker, 1992; Katz & Chard, 2000; Scheinfeld, Haigh, & Scheinfeld, 2008).

The curriculum debate over the two different approaches centers on the importance of developing children's learning processes versus teaching them conventional content and skills. These polarities represent the process-product debate. What each position fails to articulate is that in essence, for the learner, there is no content without process and there is no process without content. When learners are processing and using their inquiry and thinking skills, they are acquiring some kind of content and/or skills. The reverse is also true. When learners are acquiring content or academic skills, they are involved in some form of thinking.

> **In essence, for the learner, there is no content without process and there is no process without content.**

OUR BIG IDEAS FOR A SUCCESSFUL ACTION-BASED LEARNING ENVIRONMENT THAT ADDRESSES THE STANDARDS

The emergence of the standards movement has placed considerable pressure on both curriculum models. Major national professional organizations representing subject areas have produced lists defining the sequence of content and skill learnings for early childhood, which have been translated into current expectations for accountability. Articles and books devoted to translating these lists into performance standards and behavioral indicators continue to be published (Gronlund, 2006). Programs that ascribe to each curriculum model have been subject to the demands for proving their worth in terms of children's progress in meeting the standards.

It is our firm belief that we can demonstrate that the action-based learning environment supports children's ownership of both the content and academic skills cited in the standards. The big ideas that govern our work toward this end are:

1. Children's interests drive their learning.
2. As children pursue activities of their own choosing in interest centers, they draw on prior knowledge and skills to build understandings and increase their skills.
3. Children have intuitive knowledge for which they may not have the language to share.
4. Children's knowledge and use of academic skills is further extended through a set of connected curriculum activities.
5. Carefully crafted forms for recording assessment information and efficient procedures for organizing and disseminating the data meets the needs for accountability relative to the standards.

CHILDREN'S INTERESTS DRIVE LEARNING

Our design for embedding content and nurturing academic skill development within an action-based program rests on the assumption that the most enduring and sustaining learning for young children occurs through action and interaction while pursuing interests in an emotionally and cognitively responsive environment (Dewey, 1902; Dewey, 1938/1963; Genishi, 1992; Koplow, 1996; Piaget & Inhelder, 1969; Vygotsky, 1978).

> **The most enduring and sustaining learning for young children occurs through action and interaction while pursuing interests in an emotionally and cognitively responsive environment.**

We begin with the conviction that "interest drives learning." It is well documented that young children are serious thinkers and doers, continuously cycling between collecting facts and organizing the facts to create understandings (Chukovsky, 1968; Donaldson, 1978; Wann, Dorn, & Liddle, 1962). They gather facts directly through their senses, by watching, listening, and interacting with people and materials. What facts they collect are shaped by the cognitive characteristics of their developmental stage, their prior understandings, and their interests (Forman & Kuschner, 1983; Malcolm, 1998). When a young child first discovers that a sponge will pick up water, the information that is being collected centers on "soaking up" and "squeezing out" water. Fascination with this fact drives what seems like endless repetition of the simple set of actions of observing the absorption event and squeezing the sponge (see Photo 1.1). The awareness of the possibility of moving water from one place to another via the sponge grows slowly, even when it is demonstrated by the adult.

PHOTO 1.1

Young children's learning, as well as that of adults, begins with the acquisition of new information as they use materials and exchange ideas with others. It is followed by the process of absorbing the new facts based on prior knowledge and understandings and then using the new understandings in a variety of situations. In essence, during these early years they are building an experiential body of knowledge in the traditional content areas of science, mathematics, social studies, and literacy (Klugman & Smilansky, 1990; Monighan-Nourot et al, 1987; Reynolds & Jones, 1997).

The interest generated from children's varied experiences with materials depends upon a number of factors. First and foremost, interest probably flows from the unique characteristics of the individual child in terms of development and learning style. We cannot easily explain why there is such a wide degree of difference in children's interests which are triggered by materials. Nor do we know why the same materials will hold children's interests for different reasons. For example, when using miniature cars, some children are more fascinated with the movement of cars, sometimes "racing" or "driving" them up and down inclines, or even transforming them to flying machines. Others turn their attention to building structures to house the cars. In this case, the cars merely serve as props for construction activities.

Other sources of interest flow from exposure to different types of experiences that range from opportunities for discovery and experimentation with things in their environment to exposure to information transmitted to them by adults, siblings, peers, and various forms of media. Irrespective of the source of the interest, children are builders of their own understandings, and the materials they use to build their understandings exist in their environment.

STRENGTHENING CONTENT LEARNING

Our approach to strengthening content is grounded in the belief that the most enduring and sustaining learning for young children occurs during activities that engage and sustain their interest. It therefore follows that we need to increase our focus on identifying and capitalizing on the embedded content that shows up as they pursue their interests. It is not enough to depend on children's self-directed activities in the centers as the sole source of content acquisition. Nor can we count on children's ability to sustain important content learning provided primarily through direct instruction. Both opportunities are needed to ensure sustained and continuing learning.

> It is the constant interplay between exposure to new experiences
> and skills and time to make meaning out of the new experiences through
> one's own actions that constitutes the core of children's learning.

It is the constant interplay between exposure to new experiences and skills and time to make meaning out of the new experiences through one's own actions that constitutes the core of children's learning (Wann, Dorn, & Liddle, 1962).

Building on Prior Learning

We know that before schooling begins, much of what children learn occurs through the use of a varied collection of materials, and often with little direct instruction. Since children bring different backgrounds of experience as they enter group settings, it is important that they be provided the time to process new information gained from teacher-directed activities through their own individual lens. The way in which they process information is by using it in self-directed activities. If children do not have this opportunity, much of the content of the teacher-designed activities will go "unprocessed." Teachers will have no means of finding out how the new content is being organized, interpreted, and internalized by the children.

This commitment to supporting children's ways of learning requires that we clearly identify the key ideas in the major areas of adult content knowledge: mathematics, science, social studies, and language and literacy. Further, we need to recognize what these ideas look like in children's actions as they emerge and grow. Our adult understandings of key ideas, such as the concept that "matter/materials in our world exists in three states," is formed over a number of years with a variety of sequential experiences–in this case, beginning with being bathed as babies. As we come to understand the path through which the key ideas develop from childhood onward, we can support children's progress in developing these ideas through focused conversations and activities that extend experiences related to observed interests.

The Action-Based Program Context

The daily schedule of programs described as child-centered typically include a minimum of 50 minutes within a half-day program for children to pursue independent activity in interest centers that have a rich variety of materials well organized for children's selection and use. In addition, the schedule includes small- and total-group activities initiated by the adults that are designed to expand upon the selected interests of the children, spark new interests, and set contexts for meeting the standards. The inclusion of interest-center periods and adult-directed periods is designed to meet a broad range of learning/developmental needs in the areas of aesthetic, physical, social, cognitive, and communication (Bredekamp & Copple, 2009; Fromberg, 1995; Van Hoorn et al., 1999).

Expanding the Teaching Role

Increasing curriculum content and addressing the standards requires expanding the teaching role to help children clarify and expand the ideas they are using in their activities (Epstein, 2007). In action-based programs that are dedicated to strengthening content, the teaching role needs to serve three specific functions. The most familiar is that of *leading*. In this role, the adult transmits a large amount of social and content knowledge through modeling, demonstrating, explaining, and directing. We take the position that effective fulfillment of this role precludes the practice of teaching discrete content that is essentially not in a context that children can or will use—that is, lessons that "stand alone." However, it does not preclude direct instruction wherein children acquire the knowledge and/or skills that they want or need as they pursue program activities. For example, when children want to accurately write their names independently on a craft product, teacher-guided practice prior to writing the name serves a purpose that the child values.

A second function, which we call *seeding,* is equally familiar. This role encompasses setting up the classroom, organizing materials for use by children, and providing enrichment materials in a timely manner in order to stimulate further activity without direct instruction.

The third function is less familiar. It involves *feeding* content thinking and the development of social skills and understandings during center-time and group-time activities by engaging in authentic conversations that pick up on children's ideas and feelings (Schwartz, 2005). In our experience, the instructional strategies related to the function of feeding content learning are the most challenging for teachers. However, the interactions that take the form of feeding during interest-center periods have great potential for fostering children's thinking and increasing their knowledge and skill base. Further, these interactions set the context for introducing new curriculum experiences during group time that stimulate children to make additional connections between what they know and what they are now experiencing. Once we establish the pattern of progressively connecting the content embedded in curriculum activities to children's interests, the momentum develops for a content-rich curriculum. This approach recognizes the interdependence between learning through exposure to new experiences and actively processing the experiences for understanding by using the knowledge and skills in a variety of situations.

As children pursue activities of their own choosing in interest centers, we have the window needed to begin to understand what they know, what they are figuring out, and what they don't know in terms of the key ideas in content areas. Some of their knowledge is intuitive. Children do not yet have a conscious awareness of many of the ideas they are using, nor do they have the language to talk about them (Sophian, 1999). We can help them make some of their intuitive knowledge more explicit through conversation with adults about their ongoing activities.

SUMMARY

This book describes what we, in our work with teachers, learned as we turned our attention to developing the critical professional skills needed to prove the importance of action-based learning environments for the long-term learning of preprimary children. The required professional skills include:

- Development of fluency with key ideas and related facts in the content areas that progressively emerge in children's interactions with materials, peers, and adults.
- Recognition of the variety of behavioral indicators that illustrate children's growing understanding of the key content ideas and related academic skills that occur during self-directed activities.
- Connections between performance standards, behavior indicators, and key ideas in the content areas.
- Expansion of instructional strategies to foster children's ability to talk about their emerging ideas and understandings with both peers and adults.
- Increased familiarity with ways to extend content learning and acquisition of skills through high-interest curriculum activities.
- Increased effectiveness in documenting children's development and learning for accountability purposes.

Each of the following chapters address these important ideas. In Chapter 2, we discuss what is meant by the terms *content* and *key ideas*, and provide examples of their correlation with *the standards*. Sample lists of content and key ideas in science, mathematics, social studies, and communication arts are included in this chapter, as well as in the appendices.

Chapter 3 reviews the function and form of the three roles of the teacher—leading, seeding, and feeding—in strengthening content and academic skill acquisition. It considers teachers' roles in using key ideas in curriculum topics to shape decisions about their interactions with children in centers and the design of program activities. We explore ways to expand the feeding role of the teacher in developing conversations with children in centers as they intuitively and consciously use content ideas when pursuing interests with materials and peers. Included are many of the strategies and curriculum experiences generated by teachers to strengthen children's content learning and skill development in a high-interest context.

In Chapters 4–8 we look at how children's intuitive use of many of the content ideas and conventional academic skills typically emerge in classroom interest centers and ways in which teachers can capitalize on the opportunities to strengthen content and meet the standards. The traditional centers we selected are Block Center (Chapter 4), Water and Sand Center (Chapter 5), Manipulative Materials Center (Chapter 6), Drama Center (Chapter 7), and the Expressive Arts and Literacy Centers (Chapter 8). The use of key ideas related to strengthening content is addressed in each chapter where we describe typical activities that provide the basis for identifying and expanding content learning. We include photos and narrative descriptions of observations that reflect the vitality of center activity as well as transcripts of adult-initiated conversations that illustrate the possibilities for capitalizing on children's interests. Examples of the interplay between interests sparked by teachers at group times and interests generated by children during center activity expose further possibilities for expanding the curriculum. These illustrations of teacher-child interactions document the importance of retaining a balance between the instructional roles of *leading* and *feeding* and children's independent processing of their experiences in center activities.

In Chapter 9 we address the critical need for documenting and assessing children's progress in terms of developmental and academic standards in the action-based program and recording the information for accountability/reporting purposes. Procedures for collecting, organizing, and analyzing the data are illustrated and discussed.

Chapter 10 revisits the ideas for and challenge of expanding content and strengthening practice in an action-based learning environment for pre-primary children.

Throughout the book, we share with the readers how content emerges as children pursue their interests using a rich variety of materials provided in the interest centers of an action-based learning environment. We illustrate the many ways they show us how they are using their prior knowledge and how we can help them connect this knowledge to content ideas. We examine the possibilities for engaging them in conversation and shaping additional curriculum activities to stimulate further learning.

CHAPTER 2

Defining Content: Addressing the Challenge to Expand Content and Strengthen Skills

No man can reveal to you aught but that which already lies half asleep in the dawning of your knowledge.

—Khalil Gibran, *The Prophet*, p. 56

The focus on strengthening curriculum content in an action-based setting requires that we clarify what we mean by content and what knowledge is "dawning" in the minds of young children. Over the years, as we have worked with preprimary teachers, the continuing question we have heard is, "What is the curriculum and what content should we be teaching?" In this chapter we outline for the reader key ideas in the major content areas in order to more clearly answer this question.

THE WAY YOUNG CHILDREN LEARN

The context for strengthening curriculum content outlined in this chapter flows from our view of the way in which young children learn. Children are "fact collectors." They continuously gather an enormous number of facts, by watching, listening, and doing. As children gather facts, they organize them into concepts that become part of their growing body of knowledge in the traditional content areas of science, mathematics, social studies, and literacy. In essence, content for young children is this growing body of accumulated facts and the understandings that are constructed from the collected information. The pattern of learning begins with the acquisition of new information, through action and interaction with materials, peers, and

> In order to support children as they seek to validate or adapt their understandings, we need to be very clear about the "big ideas" in the content areas that they are using.

adults. It is followed by connecting the new facts with existing knowledge and then expanding the understandings or developing new concepts (Falk, 2009; Forman & Kuschner, 1983; Good, 1977; Piaget, 1977). Concepts are always in the process of adaptation and change as new experiences challenge prior understandings. In order to support children as they seek to validate or adapt their understandings, we need to be very clear about the "big ideas" in the content areas that they are using. Equally important is adult awareness of the progression in which the ideas grow and serves as the umbrella under which their learnings gather (Roschelle, 1995).

Expanding Content Through "Play"

Despite the current attacks on "play-based programs," the preprimary teachers with whom we worked over the years have taken a firm stand that the center-time period, which many referred to as "play time," was an essential vehicle for fostering children's development and learning. They were very familiar with the early childhood professional literature that documents how and what children learn during play as they pursue interests using materials and talking with peers (Cuffaro, 1995; Hartley, Frank, & Goldenson, 1952; Helm & Beneke, 2003; Wann, Dorn, & Liddle, 1962). In addition, the teachers were convinced that the experiences developed for group time were equally important for introducing and expanding the content associated with conventional academic subjects. They could describe many discrete learning goals and standards that were addressed during the various segments of the daily schedule, yet they were not confident that the accumulated group-time experiences combined with center-time periods adequately provided children with the content understanding and skills they needed to move on to the primary grades.

Examining a Typical Curriculum Activity

Most of the current curriculum books available for early childhood teachers are rich with methodology for nurturing discovery as well as connecting curriculum activities to their corresponding standards. Typically, these curriculum texts identify what children should be able to do, or what inquiry skills they should be developing as they pursue the suggested activity. What is missing in most of the general curriculum texts are clear statements of the key ideas young children can develop and related facts that are embedded in children's actions when they engage in the recommended activities. Without a clear view of this embedded content, teachers are not ready to initiate conversations that help children bring their intuitive knowledge to a conscious level for discussion.

A popular activity on sprouting seeds that is found in many early childhood curriculum guides usually includes a description of the materials and procedures, and suggestions on how to promote observation. Suggestions feature the use of inquiry skills to compare and examine the contents of seeds, directions on how to plant the seeds, and charts for recording observations of growth and change. Sample teacher questions for the initial segment of the activity deal with describing seeds and making predictions about speed of the germination. At later events, it is suggested that children's attention be directed to experimenting in order to discover the needs of seeds for water and light while they are germinating. The activity plan omits the listing of key ideas about germination that can be developed through focused observation and conversation that can continue during repeated experiences of sprouting seeds. These include:

1. Given proper moisture and temperature conditions, seeds sprout in a predictable pattern that can be observed: the seed coat shrivels, the roots and stems grow out of opposite ends of the seed, and ultimately the seed coat falls off, revealing a seedling.
2. Inside of seeds are the beginnings of new plants.
3. The speed of sprouting varies with different kinds of seeds.
4. The seedlings—the new plants that have emerged from the seeds—require a plant medium, adequate light, and moisture in order to continue to grow.
5. The seedlings grow and change in predictable and observable ways. They increase in size and leaves appear.
6. Seeds vary not only in physical properties but also in the plants that they will produce. They are similar in that they produce new plants.
7. The rate of plant growth varies with different kinds of plants (Martin, 2009).

Our ability to engage in activities and related conversations that will support children's knowledge-building depends a great deal upon how well the content ideas are organized in our own minds, ready for using in conversation in a timely way.

ADDRESSING THE DEFICIENCIES
IN THE EARLY CHILDHOOD STANDARDS MOVEMENT

The current standards movement, which embraces early childhood, seeks to address the need for greater consistency on curriculum content goals across the grades. Each set of standards generated by a particular group varies in the way the standards are stated. Some list facts and understandings or inquiry skills. Others refer to "Performance Standards" and "Behavior Objectives/Goals/Indicators." There is no consistent format for stating the expected outcomes. They use such terms as "understands," "uses," "recognizes," "applies the skills of," or "demonstrates," without distinguishing content learning from skill development. Many are missing explicit identification of a set of key ideas in the content areas to be developed as the core of the curriculum.

In this book, the list of content ideas that young children can begin to develop and extend are culled from the literature generated by national and state professional subject area organizations in mathematics (National Council of Teachers of Mathematics [NCTM]), in science (National Science Teachers Association [NSTA]), in social studies (National Council for the Social Studies [NCSS]), in literacy (National Council for the Teachers of English [NCTE] and International Reading Association [IRA]), and in early childhood (National Association for the Education of Young Children), as well as scholars in each of these areas.

The performance standards and the behavior indicators which we relate to the content ideas are culled, as much as possible, from the variety of state and local early childhood standards publications. Where necessary, they are adapted from these many sources. It is important for the reader to understand that many of the statements in our charts—which list key content ideas, performance standards, and behavior indicators—may be found in the resources cited. Some are adapted by the authors to make the content more usable. We are committed to providing teachers with a framework for infusing the content into curriculum activities and shaping their instructional interactions in order to demonstrate that the action-based learning environment can also meet "the standards."

> **In this book, the listing of content ideas that young children can begin to develop and extend are culled from the literature generated by National and State Professional Subject Area Organizations in Mathematics, Science, Social Studies, Literacy and Reading, and Early Childhood, as well as professional scholars in each of these areas.**

ORGANIZING TEACHER
CONTENT KNOWLEDGE

Key ideas in the content areas serve as a guide for the teacher to focus children's observations and stimulate their thinking. Coordinating the body of knowledge that we have as adults with the emergence of children's understandings presents a challenge, because we have already internalized so much of the kind of knowledge that is just beginning to take form for young children. While most teachers have a great deal of knowledge in the content areas, that knowledge is not organized for easy reference to the concepts that govern an understanding of topics.

Adult Fluency with Content

The professional goal of strengthening content in action-based settings begins with developing adult fluency with the major ideas that govern our understanding of content in the subject areas of science, mathematics, social studies, and language and literacy. Fluency means developing sufficient familiarity with the key concepts that constitute the core knowledge in the subject area, so that they are easy to draw upon for planning curriculum activities and engaging in conversation with children during these activities. It also involves recognizing the ways in which such concepts emerge as the children use the classroom resources in centers and respond to new curriculum experiences. Professional fluency with the key concepts or big ideas establishes a framework for (1) observing and interacting with children in centers, and (2) designing activities and selecting instructional strategies that capitalize on children's interests and stimulate further interest.

An analysis of the ideas that govern our understanding of liberal arts and science subjects reveals their connection to the standards. In the above discussion about the curriculum activities for sprouting seeds, the big ideas in life science deal with the life cycle of living things and diversity in nature. Specifically, (1) living things progress through a series of changes that define their life cycle, (2) the pattern of change is unique to each group of living things, and (3) there are a variety of types or classes of living things in both the plant and animal world. Multiple experiences with sprouting seeds and growing plants give children the opportunity to generate more complex understandings about these major ideas at their age level. If they are fascinated with the stages of seed sprouting, then the introduction of different kinds of seeds offers an opportunity for children to compare the attributes of a variety of seeds and recognize the similarities as well as differences in their sprouting pattern. If, on the other hand, they become fascinated with growth and change after sprouting, then the activities can open the door to noticing the

> Content idea fluency affords us flexibility in pursuing conversations with the children and choosing opportunities for creating and extending activities.

differences and similarities in the structure and growth pattern of different plants and their needs for survival.

Recognizing Content in Children's Actions

Content idea fluency affords us flexibility in pursuing conversations with the children and choosing opportunities for creating and extending activities that will stimulate them to continue to collect facts and organize those facts to adapt and/or extend prior generalizations.

In a recent activity that we observed, a small group of prekindergarten children were experimenting with the shadow phenomena using an overhead projector as the light source. They initially became very excited about the connection between the shadow and the object that cast it. After one child put a star on the projector, she moved to the screen to show her classmates her discovery: "Look, it's the star!" Another child chimed in, "Hey. There's you," as he pointed to her shadow on the left hand side of the screen. In this event, the idea that there is a direct relationship between the object casting the shadow and the shadow that is created takes form in a direct experience with the shadows cast by both the star and the child.

However, when they placed a cup on the projector the children became confused because the shadow did not resemble the profile of a cup. It merely showed up as a shadow in the shape of a circle cast by the base of the cup. One child wondered, "What happened to the cup?" In this experience, the children were on the verge of discovering another big idea: that in addition to the shape of the object, its position or orientation determines the shape of the shadow that is cast.

In order to begin to expand their initial understanding to accommodate this new discovery, the children needed to pursue their experiments with the orientation of the object—"on its side," "upside down," "turned around." Figure 2.1 lists the Key Content Ideas in the topic of shadows in the first column, and pairs them with Performance Standards and Behavior Indicators in the second column.

Identification of the progression in the development of key concepts about shadows listed in the first column helps us make decisions about how to sequentially focus children's attention on variables that affect the size and shape of shadows while they are engaged with the materials. The progression

FIGURE 2.1. Physical Science

SHADOWS

Key Content Ideas	Performance Standards and Behavior Indicators
A shadow is the darkness that is cast when light shines on an opaque object that is situated between a light source and a surface.	*Experiments with making shadows.* Makes shadows by placing different materials in the space between the light source and a surface.
The shape of the shadow is determined by the shape and position/orientation of the object casting the shadow.	*Experiments with changing a shadow shape by changing objects and position of objects that are casting the shadow.* Identifies the object casting the shadow by looking at the shadow.
The shape of a shadow changes as the angle of the light changes in relation to the surface.	*Discovers that a change in the position of the light source changes the shadow shape.* Repeatedly changes the position of the light source and points out how the shadow is changing.
The size of a shadow changes when the distance between the light source and the object casting the shadow is changed.	*Realizes that the size of shadows can be changed by moving the object or light source.* Changes the size of the shadow by changing the position of the object or the light source and explains the cause.

also guides us in making decisions about choosing activities that will draw their attention to new information and pursuing conversations that help them make connections with their prior understandings.

Strengthening content in all subject areas of science requires not only that we provide curriculum experiences that expand children's awareness of concepts, but also that we provide the language with which to exchange perceptions and ideas as they increase their experiential knowledge in the process.

KEY CONTENT IDEAS IN SCIENCE

Young children are natural scientists, continuously experimenting and discovering. Typical activities in all interest centers in the preprimary classroom

> **In the process-product equation, the inquiry skills represent the process. What children find out and figure out when they use these inquiry skills represents the content we are targeting.**

involve a great deal of science content. In this book we are using a familiar division of science into the following three branches: (1) physical science, (2) life science, and (3) earth and environmental science. Although the most common approach to defining science content in early childhood programs is to equate it with the inquiry skills listed in Figure 2.2, we believe the core ideas in the content that they uncover through inquiry are equally important. The emphasis on the use of the inquiry skills signifies the importance we place on nurturing children's ability to be active processors of their own learning. In the process-product equation, the inquiry skills represent the process. What children find out and figure out when they use these inquiry skills represents the content we are targeting.

Physical Science

Physical science is the branch of science that deals with such topics as properties of matter, the physical laws of motion, and magnetism. Children never cease to be fascinated with discovering and changing the properties of objects. A typical activity that illustrates this understanding is cooking. During an experience of mixing pudding powder with milk, several content facts surface: The powder floats on the milk; then it begins to dissolve, changing the color of the milk; and then it disappears. One concept that children

FIGURE 2.2. Science Inquiry Skills

Pose questions, seek answers, and develop solutions by:
- observing, investigating, and asking questions about objects and events in the environment,
- collecting, describing, and recording data,
- comparing, contrasting, and classifying objects and events in the environment,
- using equipment in investigation,
- making and verifying predictions,
- developing generalizations about the relationship between objects and within and between events,
- communicating observations, ideas, and understandings.

Source: Adapted from New York City Department of Education, 2003, p. 41

begin to understand is that when powders and liquids mix, the properties of both the powder and the liquid change—in this case, most notably, color and taste (Colker, 2005).

With subsequent cooking experiences, using different kinds of foods, the facts that emerge may deal with a different kind of change—for example, the change in the density and color of eggs as they are cooked. While the facts the children are collecting relate to the different attributes of the food material and forces of change, these facts connect to the first two key ideas about matter, listed in Figure 2.3; namely, the ideas that "Objects have properties that can be described, compared, and changed using different kinds of forces," and that "Objects can be grouped based on identical or similar physical properties and patterns of change of properties." In these examples, it is the properties of food materials that change when mixed or heated. Comparing and contrasting kinds of changes can become a part of ongoing conversations during activities where change is occurring. Stirring causes change in mixtures. Heat causes change in the texture and density of food materials. Physical force causes change in the shape of materials as when molding clay and cutting paper. Progressive discussions in context about observed changes and the forces that caused them build children's repertoire of knowledge that can be organized into generalizations over a period of time.

FIGURE 2.3. Physical Science

PROPERTIES OF MATTER

Key Content Ideas	*Performance Standards and Behavior Indicators*
Objects have properties that can be described, compared, and changed using different kinds of forces.	*Uses the senses to examine the physical properties of objects.* Describes and compares properties of objects and changes in properties.
Objects can be grouped based on identical or similar physical properties and patterns of change.	*Sorts and groups objects based on identical or similar physical properties.* Describes and compares the properties of sorted sets and talks about the reason for groupings.
Matter occurs in a solid, liquid, or gas state, and can change states.	*Understands that matter exists as a solid, liquid, or gas.* Experiments with changing state of materials and describes the changes.

> **Progressive discussions in context about observed changes and the forces that caused them build children's repertoire of knowledge that can be organized into generalizations over a period of time.**

Physical laws of motion evoke the same kind of fascination as the properties of matter. Children's experimentations with moving objects offer a strong testimonial to their desire to understand and control this phenomena. Typically, when they get their hands on objects that roll, they push them many different ways, discovering "what happens *when . . .*" In the block center, ramps capture the attention of many youngsters. Their discovery of the effects of gravity on an object moving down an inclined plane leads to increased efforts to control the variables that account for speed, direction, and distance. "Look, my car can go down." "Look how far it went!" "Mine is the fastest." "Yours fell off so that doesn't count." Adult familiarity with the connection between big ideas and children's actions, as noted in the behavior indicators on Figure 2.4, establishes the context to nurture their budding understanding. It leads to conversations and extended activities that can expose children to opportunities to discover the second big idea on the chart that deals with the variables of shape of the moving object and the surfaces—both the surface of the item that is moving and the surface on which it moves.

FIGURE 2.4. Physical Science

PHYSICAL LAWS OF MOTION

Key Content Ideas	Performance Standards and Behavior Indicators
A force is needed to move an object. The forces include physical force, such as physical pushing and pulling, gravity—the pull of the earth (the angle of the plane on which it is moving), moving air, and simple machines (levers, gears, pulleys).	*Observes, investigates, and asks questions about events.* Purposefully experiments with ways in which to move objects.
The speed, distance, and direction of movement of an object are dependent upon the shape and surface of the object and the surface on which it moves, as well as the force.	*Discovers that the speed, distance, and direction of movement can be controlled by using different-shaped objects and varied surface textures.* Purposefully adjusts force to control speed and direction of movement and talks about how to control or change the movement.

The kinds of investigations that take place with magnets usually consist of a series of brief actions in which children discover that some objects "stick" to magnets and others don't. This initial finding eventually can lead to the first "big idea" listed in the magnet content chart in Appendix A: "Magnetism is a force that attracts some materials and not others." However, careful planning in the selection of materials, activities, and conversation is needed to nurture an increase in understanding about magnetic force. It begins with the awareness that some objects "stick" to the magnet, and develops into a more comprehensive understanding that magnets also have the capacity to attract through space and through other materials, and finally to the awareness that they can repel other magnets. In Appendix A we have also included for reference a list of key concepts and standards for the subject areas in physical science—Physical Laws of Motion, Matter, Physical Structures, Water, Magnetism, Sound, Light, Shadows, and Moving Air.

Life Science

Life science, the branch of science that deals with plants and animals, occupies an equally important place in the discovery world of young children. The earlier discussion about sprouting seeds illustrated how the identification of the big ideas or key concepts guides the progression of activities and conversation. The content chart for life sciences in Appendix B provides similar kinds of information as the other content charts—that is, key ideas, performance standards, and behavior indicators. Study of the charts reveals that there are common threads that link plant and animal science: the ideas of diversity or variety in types of living things; differing needs for survival; and the interrelationship between structure and function of each type of living thing. Although we tend to think that preprimary children are not ready to deal with such a complex idea as the relationship between structure and function, in fact they notice it often when they observe the behavior of animals in such activities as eating, moving, or reacting to danger. The size of the mouth of animals, which is the form, determines what they can eat in order to meet their needs for survival, which serves a function. The food we put out for local birds is made up of small granules while horses eat bunches of hay. In a similar vein, children often notice the difference in size of the trunks of trees, and intuitively know that the wider the trunk (its form), the taller the tree can grow without tipping over (the trunk's function). The key content ideas listed on the chart in Appendix B offer many ways to think about helping children make connections that link these ideas during life science activities.

Earth and Environmental Science

Earth and Environmental Science is the branch of science that deals with the weather and rocks and soil. Pursuit of the content ideas listed for each of these topics included in Appendix C require a thoughtful selection of materials for experimentation. In these content areas, increased adult involvement is usually needed to extend children's collection of information and building of understandings. Although surface texture and shape are properties of rocks that can fascinate children, initial curiosity is usually satisfied by a short period of looking and touching. Stimulating further study of similarities and differences in these properties involves the provision of additional materials. For example, rolling various rocks on a bed of playdough produces imprints that give a visible image of the surface texture of different rocks for comparison and contrast and for matching the rocks with their imprints. Similarly, the key content ideas about weather require more teacher involvement in planning of activities than needed for initial experimenting in the physical sciences because children cannot experiment with and control outcomes of weather events.

KEY CONTENT IDEAS
IN MATHEMATICS

Growing understandings of content ideas in mathematics flow from all activities in the program. The connections between the development of understandings and skills in the mathematics areas of number, geometry, and measurement are very strong. Through repeated use of the skills in a variety of contexts, children realize the range of mathematical relationships that constitute content ideas (Kamii, 2000). For example, when a child counts for a purpose, as in gathering a set of precut flowers to paste on each corner of a picture he has drawn, addition and subtraction facts can emerge. The child may exclaim, "I needed eight flowers and I only got six. I need two more." The key concept the child is encountering here is that joining or separating sets creates new sets of a different quantity (Carpenter et al., 1999). Multiply these kinds of events many times over, and the skill of counting and computing becomes more stable, furthering an understanding of quantitative relationships.

Similarly, there is interdependence between the acquisition of measurement skills and the construction of understandings about measured relationships dealing with the attributes of length, weight, temperature, and time. Identical matching for length–such as cutting pieces of ribbon of equivalent length to use in a craft project—requires an awareness of the importance of baseline in linear measure. Measuring larger distances increases the complexity of the task, from simple matching for equivalent length to using a unit of measure over and over. The use of standard 3-D shapes in constructing with blocks and assembling and disassembling manipulative materials increases awareness of the properties of shape that establishes a foundation for constructing understanding of big ideas in geometry. The content and standards charts in number, geometry, and measurement coordinate the critical skills with the content ideas that emerge in the use of those skills as children pursue high-interest activities in centers and curriculum activities at group time (see Appendix D).

KEY CONTENT IDEAS IN SOCIAL STUDIES

The field of social studies is one of the more complex content areas because it represents so many bodies of knowledge. According to the National Council for the Social Studies (NCSS),

> The primary purpose of the social studies is to help young people develop the ability to make informed and reasoned decisions for the public good as citizens of a culturally diverse, democratic society and an interdependent world. (NCSS, 2004)

Of the 11 subjects that NCSS lists, the ones that we view as most relevant to early childhood programs are economics, geography, history, psychology, and sociology. The areas in which children begin to develop key ideas in each of these subjects are:

- in economics: exchange of goods and services and job roles.

    Sample Behavior Indicator: Dramatizes job roles in different kinds of business and community services.

- in geography: vehicle and people pathways, routes and distances between places, use of land surface, organization of space.

    Sample Behavior Indicator: Makes simple 3-D maps of familiar areas that define an indoor or outdoor space.

- in history: time sequences—the relationship between past, present, and future events.

    Sample Behavior Indicator: Identifies daily and weekly event sequences.

- in psychology and sociology: self-valuing, self-knowing and group membership, multiculturalism.

   Sample Behavior Indicator: Helps formulate and follow class rules.

The content charts for each of these subject areas are included in Appendix E. The ways in which to translate the development of content ideas in economics into curriculum activities within the action-based learning environment are discussed in detail in Chapter 7, "Strengthening Content in the Drama Center." Geography content emerges in Chapter 4, "Strengthening Content in the Block Center," and content within psychology and sociology pervades the whole program.

KEY CONTENT IDEAS IN LANGUAGE AND LITERACY

In an educated society, language is the vehicle for communicating information and understandings, ideas, and emotions. Children begin school with varying levels of expertise in listening to, understanding, and speaking the languages they hear at home. They also come to school with exposure to print and a growing ability to use the print they see in their environment. They have watched adults read and write and have used writing tools to make marks on surfaces.

Concerns for literacy learning during the early years have dominated curriculum designs for several decades. Of all the curriculum areas, literacy instruction has provoked the greatest discussion and is the most familiar to early childhood professionals. Much of the debate polarizes the issue. At one end is the skill-driven approach, where literacy instruction is taught through isolated lessons. At the other end is a program in which literacy learning is a developmental process where children participate in literacy activities that occur in natural contexts. In reality, neither approach exists in a pure condition. In skill-driven programs, children develop literacy skills during noninstructional periods as well as during instructional periods. In programs that do not place emphasis on drills, practice of literacy skills does occur in some activities involving direct instruction as well. Children also choose to practice many of the literacy skills that are the target of instruction in most programs, such as repeating familiar rhymes to themselves and making up new ones.

We cannot underestimate the importance of building children's expressive language competence, both oral and written, through a variety of curriculum experiences. Since children's use of both oral and written language begins with personal inventions or "approximations," the role of the teacher is to model conventional speech and writing as well as to provide additional models in the environment. Interaction and practice with these models will move the children closer to the use of a conventional or "common" language. Since the function of expressive language is communication, the goal of language and literacy instruction is to bring children to the place where they formulate what they wish to communicate and produce it so that it can be understood by others. Halliday (1973) theorizes that the function of language precedes form and that the form develops through everyday use. Therefore, it is natural that actions and gestures precede graphic, oral, and written language (Harste, Woodward, & Burke, 1984). The role of the teacher is to notice the language uses and forms that children bring to school and support their growth in moving toward the standards in ways that increase their sense of competence in communication.

The language and literacy content and standards included in Appendix F describe standards for oral communication, listening and speaking, as well as written communication, reading, and writing. Both oral and written communication put emphasis on comprehension or making meaning out of what is heard or read. In addition, it includes vocabulary development. A *key idea* on the language and literacy chart is: "The more precise the language, the more effective the communication is likely to be." This key idea indicates that one area of focus for literacy development is word meaning or vocabulary. The development of vocabulary words that (1) are unique to content, for example, in the shadow experiment, "darkness" or "opaque"; (2) feature the skills of inquiry children are using, such as "compare" or "contrast"; and (3) describe position, size, and shape, for example, "on its side," "upside down," "wider or narrower," or "darker or lighter" all contribute to greater precision in language, which adds to more effective communication.

The content in language and literacy also includes phonological awareness, print awareness, print conventions, letter-name knowledge, alphabetic principles, knowledge of text structures, comprehension of stories, and interest in books. We have not included these components in the Language and Literacy chart, not because we are unaware of their importance, but rather because the extensive emphasis on literacy learning in the early childhood years has resulted in a flood of resources that are available to teachers. Additionally, local communities have adopted different approaches to developing these skills and understandings. Irrespective of the literacy program in use in a school, the opportunities to strengthen children's literacy competence in these areas pervade the action-based learning setting.

SUMMARY

In this chapter we addressed the need to specifically outline the key ideas in the major content areas that drive decision-making and begin to answer the question "What is the curriculum?" more clearly. Children are continuously collecting information and developing skills in science, mathematics, and literacy as they become involved in manipulating, experimenting, and constructing with materials, and conversing with peers and adults in an action-based learning environment. The information they are collecting and the skills they are developing directly relate to the curriculum standards. The task of meeting the challenge to strengthen curriculum requires that the adult acquire fluency with the key content ideas that govern an understanding of the subject, and recognize these key ideas as they emerge in children's actions and conversations.

CHAPTER 3

The Teacher Role in Strengthening Content and Meeting the Standards

If we want children to truly own what they learn, there is really no other choice for teachers than to focus on enhancing children's understandings.
Beverly Falk, *Teaching the Way Children Learn*, p. 63

Children's minds should be engaged in ways that deepen their understanding of their own experiences and environment.
Lillian Katz and Sylvia Chard, *Engaging Children's Minds*, p. 4

As noted in Chapter 1, one of the overriding goals of early childhood programs has been to support social-emotional development through a variety of strategies that build children's self-esteem and provide them with the opportunity to construct their understandings of the world through play. Teachers of young children are generally strong in their skills of providing positive feedback by way of praise and social guidance during the interest-center period. They enjoy admiring children's products and often ask them to talk about the product in more detail. Additionally, they help children negotiate challenges in social relationships and the sharing of materials (Kostelnik, Soderman, & Whiren, 2007; Read, 1971).

The expansion of the teacher role from manager and nurturer to include supporter of content and skill acquisition requires the inclusion of authentic conversations with children about the content and skills that are evident in their interest-driven activities. Through this approach adults can extend their ideas, and focus their attention on new possibilities for understanding relationships within events. Jones and Reynolds (1992) reported that in their work with preprimary teachers to expand their roles, "some roles were more readily accepted than others." Further, when they sought to "encourage teachers to plan for children's learning through play" they were sometimes met with resistance (pp. xii–xiii). We approached this challenge by identifying ways in which to enter into the child's world.

In order to bring content into their engagements with children about their interests, we introduced the idea that adult conversations with children need to reflect a quest for knowledge about children's thinking and perceptions that the adult does not already have. To do this requires the asking of authentic questions—ones that seek information for which the question-asker does not already have an answer. This can take the form of sharing with the child what has been observed and raising the question whether the observation is accurate, or it can take the form of asking the child to share his or her thinking about the observed activity—how a problem was solved or what will happen next. When a child knows that a question is authentic, he or she is more willing to share thinking without wondering if the answer is right or wrong (Kohn, 2001; Schwartz, 2005). In our experience, teachers found that initiating an authentic conversation was not an easy task. The habits of praising a product and questioning to find out what a child knows were so well entrenched that changing the mode of entry to initiate a conversation was difficult. If we are to capitalize on children's emerging interests and support their ability to make connections between what they see, do, and think about, this expansion in the teaching role is necessary and important.

STEPS IN THE PROCESS OF EXPANDING THE TEACHER ROLE

As we discussed in Chapter 2, the first steps in the process of strengthening the curriculum content in the action-based learning environment involves reviewing our adult knowledge in the conventional subject areas and becoming so familiar with the key content ideas shaping each area that we are versatile with the content ideas we can use to nurture children's learning as it is emerging.

We see the next step in the process as identifying, through observations, those key content ideas that young children are discovering and using as they engage in activities of their own choosing. This observation information in turn guides us in selecting instructional strategies and designing curriculum activities that capitalize on the content ideas they are using in order to achieve the goals of strengthening curriculum and meeting the standards.

In this chapter we share with the reader the range of instructional strategies that can be used to capture and sustain children's interest in pursuing content learning and academic skill development in environments that conform with our view of "developmentally appropriate," that is, action-based emotionally responsive learning environments.

It begins with the use of observations of children's actions and conversations in interest centers as a way to better understand what they might be discovering and thinking about. It is followed by initiating and pursuing conversations with a child in a timely way to clarify initial assumptions about what we have observed. We call this teaching strategy *feeding*. Its function is to nurture on-going thinking by providing the child with the vocabulary that is needed to talk about perceptions, intentions, or ideas related to the activity in progress.

Once having clarified through conversation what a child is discovering and/or thinking about, we have several options for capitalizing on their un-derstandings and discoveries. One option is to stimulate further discoveries on the spot, either by introducing new materials, which we call *seeding*, or by offering new information or activity suggestions, which we call *leading*. A second option is to expand on the interest expressed by a child or a group of children with follow-up curriculum activities for the whole group.

It is important to note that none of these strategies are new to the profes-sional approach of early childhood. However, coordinating the use of these strategies to formulate an integrated curriculum model has posed challenges that we found needed to be addressed to reach our objective of strengthening curriculum content in an action-based program.

IDENTIFYING EMERGING KEY CONTENT IDEAS THROUGH OBSERVATION DURING CENTER TIME

Few would argue that the best access to information about what young chil-dren already know is to watch and listen to them as they spontaneously use their knowledge and skills in activities that capture their interest (Beaty, 1986; Wann, Dorn, & Liddle, 1962).

The extensive literature on ways of studying and assessing children's de-velopment and learning serves as a strong testimonial to the fact that observ-ing children in action is not a new phenomenon in early childhood classrooms (Almy & Genishi, 1979; Boehm & Weinberg, 1996; Good & Brophy, 2008; Jablon, Dombro, & Dichtelmiller, 2007; Monighan-Nourot, Scales, & Van Hoorn, 1987). Our context for identifying emerging key ideas rests in capital-izing on the way that young children learn. As noted in Chapter 2, they are "fact collectors." They gather an enormous number of facts continuously, by watching, listening, and doing. Once collected, the facts are organized in some way to generate ideas and understandings that serve as their growing body of knowledge in the traditional content areas. When we watch them in action and listen to their interactions with peers and other adults, we can be-gin to identify the key ideas they are generating by noticing how they experi-ment with materials and solve problems in their activities. The teachers with

> Few would argue that the best access to information about what young children already know is to watch and listen to them as they spontaneously use their knowledge and skills in activities that capture their interest.

> **The daily center-time period affords the most consistently reliable opportunity to observe the emergence of those key ideas that seem to be taking shape in children's minds.**

whom we worked found that the most comfortable way to become familiar with identifying content, as it showed up in children's actions, was to use the lists of key ideas discussed in Chapter 2 and listed in detail in the appendices as a reference while observing during the interest-center period.

The daily center-time period affords the most consistently reliable opportunity to observe the emergence of those key ideas that seem to be taking shape in children's minds. Our clues come from noticing the ways in which children use materials, reflecting their understandings of "how things work" and the relationship between actions and outcomes. Their activity may be primarily (1) at the discovery level, wherein they are picking up new information or skills, (2) at the practice level, where they are testing the validity of ideas that are being formulated, and/or practicing skills, or (3) at the application level, where they may be applying ideas and skills to unique situations. Each of these levels in the learning process has unique characteristics. Although it is not possible to read the minds of young children in action, they usually provide many clues that reveal whether they are:

- *Collecting Information.* Investigating "what happens when?" leads to the discovery of relationships within an event they are creating. For example, children find out about change in color when repeatedly mixing tempera paints, such as red and white. Through repetition of actions, initial discoveries become part of the knowledge base. In Photo 3.1, the child began with painting a circle of red, and then added white, which created pink. He repeated this action a number of times before trying the same event with two other colors. Only after a child has verified information with a number of trials can that information serve a purposeful use in an activity as when painting a picture.
- *Validating a Discovery and/or Practicing a Skill.* Skill practice appears when a child does the same task over and over again, such as repeatedly using magnetic letters to replicate one's name or counting and recounting beads on a necklace that has just been strung, validating discoveries through repeated testing.
- *Using Their Content Knowledge in Seeking to Solve a Problem with Materials.* Young children's problem solving has many faces, but it is most often reflected in adjusting actions to achieve a result, such as changing the position of a block so that the structure will not fall down, or wiping the edge of a paintbrush before use to avoid dripping.

PHOTO 3.1

In addition to identifying key ideas, it is important to take note of which of these three activity levels is reflected in the child's activity.

INITIATING AND EXTENDING CONVERSATION DURING CENTER TIME

The information obtained through observation combined with prior knowledge about the observed children informs decisions about developing conversations designed to help them bring to conscious awareness the ideas that they have been using intuitively. The purpose of this step in the process is to encourage the child to put perceptions and thoughts into words through spoken language.

Initiating a Conversation

The primary strategy for initiating conversation is to confirm what the adult has observed in the child's actions related to content ideas. As noted earlier, the actions of the child might reflect efforts to (1) discover and rediscover properties of objects or relationships between objects and events, (2) apply what they know to solve a problem, or (3) practice a skill. While the most common way to initiate conversation is to ask a question, this strategy often proves unsuccessful. Such questions as "What are you making?" or

> **The primary strategy for initiating conversation is to confirm what the adult has observed in the child's actions related to content ideas.**

"How did you figure that out?" are frequently met with silence or one-word answers, "I don't know" or "I just did." These limited answers are due in part to the fact that children's perceptions and thoughts have not been sufficiently formulated in terms of language. The ability to transform intuitive thinking into spoken language is limited by the lack of a conscious awareness of the ideas in use and/or vocabulary to share it (Sophian, 1999). If the child does not have the ability to convert intuitive ideas into words, then our challenge becomes one of how to support the clarification of understanding and provide the language for continuing a conversation.

In the place of asking a question, we took the approach of seeking to confirm the adult's observation of a child's actions and embedded content initially using a validation statement followed by a think-aloud. A validation statement describes an observed action. This approach requires an entry statement that not only specifies the content that appeared to be in use, but also the kind of learning in process. For example, when a child repeatedly drops rocks and other materials into a basin of water without varying the actions, it is most likely that this is an information-collecting event. In this case, validating the observed content is probably limited to describing the child's inquiry process. Nevertheless, it fulfills the function of *feeding* the learning by increasing a child's vocabulary resources for use in conversation. A teacher might say to a child:

> *"I noticed that while you were placing these materials in the water, one at a time you were very interested in watching what happens, whether they float or sink."*

This kind of conversational entry supplies the child with some words needed to talk about what he or she is noticing related to floating and sinking. The child may respond with a more detailed observation, such as:

> *"Yes, this one floats and this one doesn't."*

Then the teacher may offer a think-aloud statement that encourages further action or stimulates the collection of more information.

> *"I wonder if this one that floated will always float or if it will sink sometimes."*

In contrast, when a child with greater experience with floating and sinking objects is more purposefully testing his or her notions about floating and sinking, we can focus on stimulating further inquiry:

> *"I noticed that you put the objects that sink in one pile and those that floated in another pile. I wonder if these two in the sinking pile will sink at the same speed."*

This entry combines the two approaches, *feeding* by seeking validation of observed actions, and *leading* by thinking aloud to nurture discovery. Familiarity with key ideas and content sequences noted in the appendices guides the choice of conversational focus intended to strengthen content learning while children are engaged with materials and peers.

In the next vignette, which occurred in the manipulative materials center, the conversational entry captured the child's problem-solving action.

> *Observed Child Activity.* A child was working at assembling the roof of a structure using magnetic triangular shapes. The first few times she tried to place the last triangle on the roof of the structure, it kept falling because she neglected to align the magnetic edges. When she finally figured out how to align this last piece and it stayed in place, she patted it and laughed quietly to herself (see Photo 3.2).
>
> *Teacher Entry to Conversation.* "I was watching how you tried to finish the roof on your house by putting the third magnetic triangle piece on the top and it kept falling off. Then you carefully put it on so that all the magnetic edges of the triangle touched other magnetic edges and then it stayed. And you were so happy that you laughed."

> **Familiarity with key ideas and content sequences noted in the appendices guides the choice of conversational focus intended to strengthen content learning while children are engaged with materials and peers.**

PHOTO 3.2

In this vignette, the teacher elected to confirm her observation of the problem-solving actions by validating how the child figured out how to complete the structure—aligning all the edges. What is important here, in terms of strengthening content, is that the teacher brought into the conversation that the edges of a magnet need to be aligned with the edges of another magnet in order for them to attract and hold together.

In a different event in the manipulatives area a teacher reported that, when he observed a child creating a single alternating pattern with pegs on a peg-board, he chose to validate the color pattern the child had made.

> *Observed Child Activity:* First Alicia collected a group of red pegs, and then a group of blue pegs, keeping the groups separate. Next, she placed a blue peg at the beginning of one row, then a red peg next to it, and continued the single alternating pattern across the row. When she ran out of red pegs in her sorted collection, she reached into the container and grabbed the first peg that she touched, a yellow one, and placed it on the row. She looked at it for a few seconds, removed it, and began searching in the container. She retrieved a few red pegs and continued the pattern to the end of the row. At this point she reviewed her work from the beginning to the end of the row, touching each peg, silently repeating, "blue-red." As she sat there, she declared to no one person in particular, "Look what I made."
>
> *Teacher Entry to Conversation:* "I noticed that after you placed the blue and red pegs in a row, you went back to the beginning and named them in order by color like this: "blue-red, blue-red, blue-red, blue-red . . ."
>
> *Child Response:* "Yeah." The child then repeated the action of pointing to and labeling the blue-red pattern.
>
> *Teacher Response:* "You know, if I were to give your pattern a name, I think I would call it a *blue-red* pattern. What do you think?"
>
> *Child Response:* Looked at the teacher for a short moment, nodded in agreement and declared "Yeah. Blue, red, blue, red."

In this event, the teacher chose to initiate the conversation with a confirming statement, dealing with the repetition of the color sequence. She followed with a think-aloud response that led the child to focus on the repeated unit which defined the pattern. For further information about the key content ideas on this topic see the chart heading entitled "Algebra" in Appendix D.

As illustrated here, there is a language pattern for initiating conversation that fulfills the function of seeking to confirm the teacher understanding of the content and skills a child seems to be using. The phrases that serve this purpose are:

- I noticed that you . . .
- I saw you do . . . when . . .
- As I watched, you created a . . . by . . .

This form of conversational entry communicates genuine adult interest in child activities.

Attentive Pause: Waiting for the Child to Respond

After initiating a conversation, an *attentive pause* lets the child know that the teacher is extending an invitation to have a conversation about the current activity. It provides the child with "think time." If the validation statement is not met with some kind of response, then it probably did not connect with the child's intuitive thinking. In that case, an alternate confirming statement might be appropriate, or more teacher observation time is needed.

Continuing the Conversation

If the validating statement successfully reflects what the child is thinking about, then it is likely to provoke a verbal response. In the floating-sinking vignette described above, if the child pursued the idea of comparing the speed of two sinking objects, the teacher may choose to encourage an extension of the inquiry with additional objects placed in the collection of "objects that sink." If the child continues the initial pattern of testing to find out whether an object sinks or floats, then the teacher may introduce the idea of predicting by wondering out-loud whether a newly introduced object will sink or float. In the patterning vignette, if the child responded to the adult focus on reaffirming the single alternation pattern by agreeing with a nod, and taking out more pegs, then the adult might inquire whether the child plans to continue making patterns with this new collection, and if so, what will be the name of the new pattern.

In each of these instances, adult knowledge about the developmental progression in expanding content ideas serves as a guide for extending a conversation that can strengthen the content learnings embedded in the activity.

Expanding on the Child's Response

The options for the teacher in responding to a child after the initial conversation range from:

- *asking questions for greater clarity* about the use of the product: "What are you going to do with . . . ?"

> After initiating a conversation, an *attentive pause* lets the child know
> that the teacher is extending an invitation to have a conversation about
> the current activity.

- *asking questions to find out about the next set of actions:* "Are you planning to add more balloons to your clown picture?"
- *sharing information and/or resources* related to the product/process: "There are different kinds of bridges. Some bridges are just for people, others are for vehicles, and some are for both people and vehicles."
- *making suggestions:* "You might want to try . . . ," "I wonder what would happen if . . ."

Exiting the Conversation

The function of the exit strategy is to confirm the discussion and express interest in following up, either by revisiting the area or pursuing the conversation with other members of the class group. For example, "I'm really interested in finding out how your building will look when it is done. Call me when you are finished, and I'll come back. Maybe we can take a picture of it to share with the others at group time."

The timing of the ending of the conversation leading to the adult exit is equally important. Ending too soon leaves the child in a position of not having finished exchanging ideas. Remaining too long diverts the child from returning to the activity. Supporting the ongoing activity of the child requires recognizing that moment when the child's interest in talking is waning, and she or he seems to want to "swing back into action."

We discovered that as teachers became more aware of different roles they could use with the children, they realized that the types of interactions they were having during center time began to have considerably more content and a richer language base. Additionally, children were initiating more conversations about what they were doing and what they had done, opening the door for even more emphasis on their process–product connections. The following example of this change in the nature of the dialogue illustrates the teachers' observations of the change in children's involvement with content.

The class had just spent a couple of weeks on a unit about farms and farm animals. After completing a structure in the block area, a kindergarten child sought out the teacher to share that he and his friend had made a farm for the animals. The cows had a big yard because there were a lot of them, and the pigs had only a small yard because they were littler than cows and there were only three pigs. As the conversation progressed, it moved to the idea that, in addition to the barnyard, cows needed a barn, a place to stay indoors, especially when the weather was very bad. The two children were stimulated by that idea and proceeded to talk about how large to make the barn before building it.

As the teacher observed the children's actions and engaged in conversation with them, she became aware of the fact that the children were realistically dealing with mathematical ideas about number, size, and area as they pursued their interest in farms, and that they had the vocabulary to talk about it.

THE USE OF RECORDING FORMS FOR PROFESSIONAL REFLECTION

Developing the skill of initiating conversations to strengthen content during center time poses the greatest challenge to teachers. Figure 3.1 offers teachers a way to keep a record of their conversations for review and reflection independently and with peers. The sections provide space for: (1) making notes on the observation of a child's actions and talk during an activity; (2) the identification of content concepts emerging in the activity and selection of focus for conversation; (3) a record of the entry statement; (4) reminder to use a pause, to give the child a chance to think about the teacher's comment; (5) a record of child's response and follow-up conversation; and finally (6) a record of exit remarks.

Teachers found that the recording form helped them sharpen their skills. First, it reminded them of the importance of observing before entering into conversation. Second, it focused their thinking on identifying emerging content to serve as a frame for conversation. Third, they thought it was valuable as a resource for expanding curriculum activities. As a result, a second page was added to the recording form for brainstorming on follow-up activities for group time and for adding additional materials to the centers to extend content learning. Sharing sessions among teachers about using these records of interaction helped to clarify how to initiate and extend conversation.

EXPANDING THE CURRICULUM WITHIN THE CENTERS

As children evidenced continued interest in a content topic, teachers identified several different routes to nurture and extend that interest within the center. One route was through seeding the centers with the addition of resources such as concrete materials, books, and photos. This strategy adds to the resources available for experimentation, creation of products, and drama. It also can stimulate activities without direct interaction with the teacher.

FIGURE 3.1. Record of Observations and Interactions

Description of activity in progress:　　　　Date:_____
Child(ren)_____　　　　Center and materials_____
Observed actions and conversation: Attach photograph and work samples.
Identification of the content that the child seems to be using in the process of the activity: Subject:_____ Key Idea(s):_____   Subject:_____ Key Idea(s):_____
Teacher entry statement:
PAUSE
Child's response and follow-up conversation:
Strategies used to further the content in the center: Process questions, think-aloud, sharing adult experiences or information, explanations, addition of text and additional resources.
Gracious exit from center activity:

This figure is available for free download and printing on the Teachers College Press website: www.tcpress.com

Another route was the use of the *leading* strategy, adding new content during discussions with the children in a particular center. If the youngsters were pursuing an interest in constructing houses, introducing a collection of pictures of houses and homes for discussion purposes serves as a stimulus for building different kinds of structures. In this approach, the teacher has selected the curriculum focus and is guiding the conversation.

EXPANDING THE CONTENT THROUGH GROUP-TIME ACTIVITIES AND THEMES

Group-time activities are the most familiar and comfortable context for developing content and skills with young children. Early childhood teachers have developed considerable expertise in fulfilling the leading roles, designing and implementing daily total group activities that launch new interests as well as feature the learning goals specified in the standards. As noted at the start of Chapter 2, the teachers often expressed concern that the content in daily teacher-directed activities did not show up in center-time periods. This means that the new content provided in group time had little or no meaning to the children, as indicated by the fact that they were not using it in ways that led to ownership during center time.

Although units and themes are an important part of the ongoing curriculum, what is so often missing is a set of clearly identified key ideas to be developed and nurtured during theme activities.

In our view, it does not matter whether a theme or topic is generated and captured in group time or through conversation in the interest centers. What matters is that children's continued interest leads to the pursuit of key ideas. This, in turn, leads to an increase in their functional knowledge base and the skills needed to continue learning. Achievement of this goal requires that the teacher add several new strategies to the teaching role. These include:

1. identifying key ideas for the topic or theme that children are likely to pursue, along with a vocabulary word list. The key ideas in the content charts in the Appendices can help in the brainstorming phase of identifying content ideas for a topic or theme;
2. seeding the centers with materials and teacher-designed tasks that continue to stimulate children to explore, experiment, and create in the topic area;

> Although units and themes are an important part of the ongoing curriculum, what is so often missing is a set of clearly identified key ideas to be developed and nurtured during theme activities.

3. utilizing observations to plan conversations with children in interest centers that will feed their growing understandings.

Figure 3.2 shows a theme planning form for developing curriculum sequences as topics and/or themes, beginning with the identification of a content focus.

A Guide for Planning and Implementing Themes, along with a sample of a plan for the topic of *shoes*, appears in Appendices G and I. These tools illustrate how thinking about and planning for an integrated curriculum theme can be promoted.

ASSESSING AND DOCUMENTING CHILDREN'S LEARNING

Another long-established role of the teacher is to assess and document children's learning. One generally accepted function of assessment is to drive instructional decision-making not only pertaining to an immediate event but also in terms of long-term planning. An equally important function is for accountability purposes, which we discuss in Chapter 9. In this chapter, we consider the links between ongoing assessment, planning and use of documentation to foster children's collection of information, understanding of content ideas and skill development.

At the core of our work to strengthen content and skills to meet the standards is observation of children's learning as it occurs in an action-based environment in order to inform instructional decisions. Many of these decisions for nurturing children's learning occur in the process of working with them—that is, "on-the-spot decisions" shaped by observations of the moment. These moments of observation and interaction provide an accumulation of information that helps shape long-term planning for meeting the needs of individual children as well as the class group.

Useful analysis of the observation information collected over a period of time requires a plan for organizing the information. Recordings in the form of anecdotal notes—a popular approach—often proves difficult to analyze in terms of a child's content understandings because of the narrative form in which it is recorded. Another approach is to record information directly onto predesigned forms that document children's developing content knowledge and coordinate the information with the child's inquiry skills in a specific subject area. The advantage of having a predesigned recording system is the clarity of the information collected. Take, for example, the performance goals in the area of matter in the physical sciences. A recording form that lists the sequential series of behaviors that show evidence of increasing knowledge and understanding about the properties of objects and

FIGURE 3.2. Focused Curriculum Planning Sheet

Focus/Theme/Topic: _____

Key Concepts:	
Key Vocabulary:	
Curriculum Plans	*Performance Standard and Behavior Indicator*
Group Time	
Launch Activities:	
Follow-up Activities:	
Read-Alouds and Shared Reading:	
Music/Gross Motor Activities:	
Center Time	
Independent Center Activities:	
Adult-Designed Center Activities:	
Culminating Activity	
Celebrating by sharing with family, other classes, and interested adults:	

This figure is available for free download and printing on the Teachers College Press website: www.tcpress.com

changes in properties can facilitate an orderly compilation of information. Figure 3.3 gives a sample of the first two items on an observational record that we piloted with several groups of teachers. The complete text of this recording form for observations of children's emerging understandings of physical science content is found in Appendix N. Note that there are two columns, one for noting children's use of content ideas during naturally occurring events at center time, and the other for noting the use of these ideas in teacher-designed activities. Since our goal is for children to internalize their understandings so that they can be used in a variety of situations, the second column provides a place for entry of observations at this more developed level of understanding and skill, wherein children apply content and skill knowledge in a task designed by another person.

Teachers reported that the use of this kind of recording form was helpful. They were able to focus their observations and then analyze the data to identify patterns of children's strengths and needs. For example, some children evidenced a need for increased verbal stimulation and vocabulary to strengthen oral language communication about the properties of objects. Others needed an increased variety of materials with which to experiment with changes in the properties of objects and the forces used to change them. This information in turn guided planning for seeding and feeding center activities as well as leading curriculum activities for the whole class group around these key ideas. Assessment in this context allowed for planning both individual and small-group interactions with high-interest materials that

FIGURE 3.3. Observational Record: Physical Science

CHILD'S NAME_____

	Naturally Occurring Event	*Date*	*Teacher-Designed Activity*	*Date*
Observes and talks about physical properties of objects	Specify: objects and properties		Specify: objects and properties	
Compares and contrasts properties of objects	Specify: objects and properties		Specify: objects and properties	

addressed developmental levels in the cognitive, linguistic, social-emotional, and academic content and skill areas.

Another assessment strategy involves the process of displaying collections of children's work that reflects their learning in a variety of ways (Chalufour & Worth, 2004). Typical examples are:

- photographs of children actively involved as learners in classroom activities and on trips,
- photographic records of topic and theme activities,
- displays of children's products on bulletin boards, in centers, and in book collections,
- collections of artifacts from theme and project activities,
- adult recordings of children's narratives in the form of pictographs,
- planning lists generated by the children for curriculum activities.

As children and adults revisit photographs and narratives of such experiences as constructing a tall tower or visiting a local dairy, they literally re-experience the learning in greater depth. They become aware of more of the critical elements of the experience as they relive it and talk about it with their peers and teachers. This kind of documentation provides the opportunity for children to increase their understandings of and appreciation for what they have learned and the skills they have acquired. In essence children are a part of the assessment process.

SUMMARY

In conclusion, the interactions between teachers and children during center and/or group time set the context for introducing new curriculum experiences. They stimulate children to make additional connections between what they know and what they are now experiencing. Once we establish the pattern of progressively connecting the content embedded in curriculum activities to children's interests, the momentum develops for a content-rich curriculum. This approach recognizes the interdependence between exposure to new experiences sparked by others and the individual processing of these experiences in self-directed activities to achieve understanding.

This chapter provided an overview of the teaching role that serves the needs for embedding content and nurturing academic skill development within an action-based program. The road to this role expansion begins with developing fluency with the key ideas in the content areas and professional skill in recognizing evidence of these key ideas appearing in children's self-directed activities. Once potential content has been identified, it needs to be coordinated with observed interests, learning style, knowledge, and skills of the child in order to select the most promising focus for conversation, *feeding* the content. The conversation may be initiated through a confirming statement or think-aloud statement followed by a *pause* to give the child "think time." The conversation then continues based on the child's response. Finally, it ends with a "graceful exit" by the adult, while the child continues the activity.

Each of the components of this process of initiating and extending conversation brings content into stronger visibility and sets a course for designing themes, units, and topical studies of high interest to children in a recursive way. In order for investigations structured by the adult to feed children's learning, it is necessary to achieve a balance between *leading* activities by the adult and the self-directed activities of the children in centers that are *seeded* with the resources to relive and expand the new experiences. The following chapters elaborate on what this approach looks like in action in the interest centers.

CHAPTER 4

Strengthening Content
in the Block Center

Fascination with blocks and construction materials begins in toddlerhood as children discover the endless possibilities of piling, stacking, lining up, and building with any block or construction material that becomes available. Blocks and the props we put into the block center invite children to manipulate and explore possibilities with the materials to discover their properties and make constructions. Photos 4.1 and 4.2 illustrate the range of children's use of blocks, from the initial collecting and piling actions to the building of increasingly complex structures through which dramatic scenes unfold.

The movement from the indiscriminate piling to purposeful building of structures generally follows an invariant route but varies in terms of pace (Johnson, 1933). The pace is influenced by learning style and prior experiences. Roschelle (1995) alerts us to the collection of research that documents that what children already know and understand establishes the context for what they can learn from new experiences.

PHOTO 4.1

PHOTO 4.2

> Roschelle (1995) alerts us to the collection of research that documents that what children already know and understand establishes the context for what they can learn from new experiences.

Youngsters with a broader set of life's experiences bring many more possibilities to their use of the block materials. Those who have had less exposure to community life and adult stimulation usually need more time and stimulation before discovering the variety of possibilities for using blocks as a medium for learning. This means that pace can be stimulated by exposure to a rich set of curriculum activities. It further leads to the idea discussed in earlier chapters, that we can no longer depend solely on what children bring to and learn from using materials their own way. We are now challenged to take advantage of the opportunities they present to us to help them expand the content and skill learning that is emerging.

It has been well documented over the years that providing children with time to work with blocks and ancillary materials in the block center allows them the opportunity to develop in the four domains of learning: physical, social-emotional, cognitive, and creative-aesthetic. Historically, much has been written about the many ways in which children use blocks to investigate mathematical relationships, experiment with scientific concepts, and express their social studies understandings through dramatization (Chalufour & Worth, 2004; Erikson, 1972; Hirsch, 1974; Lowenfeld, 1967).

Yet there remains a pervasive question: How can we interact with children in the block center to strengthen content knowledge and understandings and support academic skill development in a way that capitalizes on their expressed interests? Our work over the years with preprimary teachers in recognizing the content bedded in the children's actions has helped us uncover more about how to initiate conversations that focus children's awareness of and thinking about the content-related concepts they are using.

There is little question that a considerable amount of content is used intuitively by the children as they mature in their use of blocks. Take for example Photo 4.3, in which the child created a road, or more specifically a vehicle pathway. Study of the photo reveals that there are mathematical ideas in use, as well as geographic content. Ideas from geometry are reflected in the shape of the road created by curved and straight blocks. Measurement and number thinking is reflected in the placement of blocks of identical length, which were used to create a detour by changing the path on the road leading to the small stop sign. When the teacher approached, the child drew her attention to the stop sign, pointing to the end of the roadlike construction and explaining that it was there "because there was no more road." As he explained this, he demonstrated what he meant by reversing the direction

PHOTO 4.3

of the car he was "driving" to return along the roadway. In this activity, the child, through his construction and conversation, shared with the adult his understanding about the function of a stop sign and the message it conveys. His spontaneous sharing of his ideas opened the door for further conversation about traffic controls, a major topic in both geography and sociology, and the rules of community living. This child's understandings connect to the first key content idea in sociology and psychology cited in Appendix E, "Social Studies Content and Standards," paraphrased here:

Key Content Ideas	*Performance Standards and Behavior Indicators*
A major attribute of a democratic society is that policies and rules balance the rights of individuals with the rights of a group.	*Understands the importance of being a responsible member of a group and the standards necessary for a group to function successfully.* Helps formulate and follow class rules. Talks about rules in the neighborhood, such as waiting for the "walk" sign at stoplights.

Photo 4.2, shown earlier in the chapter, shows children's interpretation of the White House, inspired by the presidential election television reports. This structure offers more choices for conversations about topics in history and geography. In history, there is an opportunity to help children make connections between the change in leadership in our country, and the changes that have occurred in leadership in games and special class activities. Further, cultural rituals, such as hanging an American flag on important public buildings, allows us to recognize such buildings in our community. In geography, consideration of the location of the White House and surrounding structures leads to discussion about the geographic attributes of a given area. This in

turn can stimulate activities to find out more about the geographic attributes of the local area. In this particular classroom a theme about public buildings and services in the local neighborhood was launched.

Photo 4.1 offers the least opportunity for opening conversation on content because the child is just at the initial stages of "getting to know" blocks and we have few clues as to the kinds of information she is collecting. We may make a statement here about shapes of the blocks in the pile, "I see three cylinders, one curved block, and lots of straight blocks in your collection."

A block center that is well stocked with a kindergarten set of wooden blocks and a variety of props serves as the vehicle for promoting children's thinking as they engage in construction activities and use their structures to reenact experiences through drama. Teacher seeding of the center with additional props, such as miniature vehicles and animals, often influences the ideas that children develop and use.

STAGES OF BLOCK BUILDING

As illustrated in the photographs at the beginning of this chapter, children progress through stages in their use of blocks as a medium for learning. What they learn through the use of blocks is dependent upon the stage and therefore guides our decision on the focus of interaction with them to strengthen content awareness. In general, children begin the process by learning about the properties of the materials. After they become familiar with their properties, they begin to use them in more complex and technically advanced ways. Ultimately, blocks serve as tools to reconstruct important parts of their environment, which in turn leads to dramatizing familiar events and roles in their lives and to pursuing new ideas (Fromberg, 1995; Smilansky, 1968; Vygotsky, 1978).

The stages described in Figure 4.1 define the general progression in constructing with blocks and important facts children collect at each stage. From the very first experience with blocks, children are comparing and contrasting the properties of blocks, discovering similarities and differences in weight, shape, and size. As the blocks are manipulated, the measurement comparisons as well as the physical properties capture their attention. Each stage in the development of block-building listed in the first column provokes particular kinds of information-collecting through inquiry that successively leads to an increased understanding of the way in which the properties of blocks determine how they may be used in constructions. The second column of the chart identifies facts children collect through their actions and related understandings. It offers clues for initiating and extending conversations with a content and process focus.

FIGURE 4.1. Stages of Block-Building

STAGE OF BLOCK-BUILDING*	CONTENT LEARNING
Progression of Children's Actions in Using Blocks	**Facts Children Collect Through Their Actions**
Stage 1. Collecting and piling. Informally examines blocks through manipulation; does not use for construction. Identifies properties such as shape, size, weight, density, and surface texture. See Photo 4.1	• Wooden blocks vary in size, shape, and weight. • Foam blocks differ from wooden blocks in density, weight, rigidity, and surface texture.
Stage 2. Lining up and stacking. Creates rows of blocks horizontally or vertically on a single plane. See Photo 4.4	• Size of block faces, surface shape, and alignment affect balance on the vertical but not on the horizontal plane.

Stage 3. Constructing enclosures and bridges.
  • horizontal space-enclosing
  • vertical space, bridging using two blocks to support a third block.
 	
See Photo 4.5
	• Length of blocks in opposite positions need to match when enclosing or bridging space.
	• Unit blocks are based on a linear proportion 1:2:4. Two of one size matches the next larger size in length.

Stage 4. Making complex structure on both horizontal and vertical planes. See Photo 4.6	• Shape, size, position, and arrangement of blocks affect stability and balance. • Architectural features of symmetry and patterns affect the design.
Stage 5. Recreating familiar attributes of the environment; using such props as vehicles, people, and animals. See Photos 4.7 and 4.8	• Structures have unique attributes that distinguish them from one another, e.g., roadways, homes, farmyards.
Stage 6. Using constructions and accessories as props for dramatization activity: zoo, farm, shopping center, vehicles. See Photo 4.2	• Structures serve as realistic props for dramatizing and reconstructing prior experiences. And theme-related content in social studies or science.

Source: The stages are abstracted from Hirsch, 1974: Appendix 1, pp. 101–104

Conversations about content in Stage 1, where children are just finding out the basic information about blocks, are primarily limited to comparing the shapes and sizes, and perhaps matching identical blocks–for example, "I see you put the two larger blocks together and the two smaller blocks together." or "I noticed how you moved the larger block next to the smaller block."

In Stage 2, children's curiosity drives them to experiment with how the blocks fit together, as illustrated in Photo 4.4. When children line up blocks end on end and side to side, they discover more about the number of faces or surfaces on a block and how these faces vary in size of surface area. Note that this child has used most of the shapes available and has placed them in different positions related to each other. The possible conversational entries might deal with how the many different shapes are lined up on the floor, or how the shapes fit together. For example, "I noticed how you worked at fitting the arched blocks on top of the cylinders here in the middle of your building."

Stage 3 ushers in the appearance of structures that enclose space, vertically, resembling a window, and horizontally, resembling a fenced-in area. At this stage, equivalent lengths and spacing take on much more importance. Photo 4.5 is an example of the beginning level of bridging, a very simple structure. Conversation at this level can focus on the opening created by the bridge, or the way the bridging block fits across the span. For example, "I was watching how you positioned the cylinders so that you could bridge them with the unit blocks. And now, two of those three bridges are holding another block on top."

Photo 4.6 shows a well-developed construction representing Stage 4. It shows the use of cylinders for bridging at the base of a structure. In addition, there is a middle bridge resting on the two base bridges. There are two enclosures without filled in space and what appears to be a partial enclosure filled in with small blocks.

PHOTO 4.4

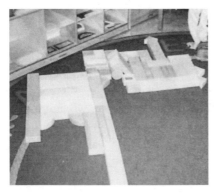

PHOTO 4.5

PHOTO 4.7

PHOTO 4.6

The options for selecting an entry statement to launch conversations involve the structural elements, the use of the cylinders for the base of two bridges, the spacing requirements for creating the middle bridge, or the vertical stack where she used two different lengths of blocks. If the teacher was able to observe the child solving a problem during the construction, then the entry statement may include a reference to the process as well as the product. For example, "I noticed that after you made the first two bridges resting on top of the cylinders, you had to figure out how to make this middle bridge using the two bridges you already had. I saw you move them closer together to make the middle bridge."

At Stage 5, constructions become more complex and realistic. Children increasingly utilize accessories as props and attach more meaning to them. At Stage 5, the beginnings of dramatization often flow from their media experiences. They create a platform for some kind of action, but the actions are brief and the construction adjustments are frequent. Photo 4.7 represents the last in a series of adjustments this child made in patterning the blocks and then patterning the figures as he included them in the structure.

Each time he picked up a figure, he moved it in some kind of drama action before placing it in ordered relationship to the other figures. First he placed one figure in each section and then proceeded to increase the number to two in each section. The observable drama was limited, therefore it is unknown how much drama was going on in the child's head. Consequently, the safest entry to initiate conversation is one that talks about quantity and patterns: "I noticed that there are three figures in each set" or, with regard to the placement of the figures and blocks, "I see that you put two figures on each block segment and one figure in front; you also put one triangular block at the top of each rectangular block."

Most often at Stage 5, blocks become a tool for recreating community buildings and environmental locales that reflect an interest in better understanding the relationships of structures within a community. In Photo 4.8, the two youngsters have constructed an enclosure for parking different kinds of vehicles. Observations of the process would have revealed the relative importance of the construction and the potential drama associated with it. This in turn would offer clues to the content that might be selected for a conversation entry. For example, "I see you have placed four different kinds of vehicles in this enclosed area. They all look like construction vehicles. Am I right?"

During the process of building structures, many problems arise that require the builder to focus on mathematical relationships in number, geometry, and measurement, and scientific understandings in order to achieve balance and stability. The children's efforts frequently reveal their intuitive understanding of a problem and ability to solve it. Often the children will invite the adult into conversation, which then leads to helping them clarify their ideas and expand their thinking.

Ultimately, at Stage 6, children plan and build structures that they intend to use for dramatic purposes, as shown in Photo 4.9. In this photo the children are dramatizing their version of a "garbage factory" in which they are using garbage trucks to dump garbage and using woodworking tools to adapt parts of the structure. The social studies content deals with concepts such as job roles, community service activities, and building maintenance. At this stage children are more likely to be interested in the drama than in the actual building. A simple structure can be used to create an elaborate scenario. The focus for content conversation would be around the drama in the social studies arena and can be theme related (e.g., "I noticed that John is driving the garbage truck and Sam is dumping the garbage. That's the same way the garbage collectors work when they pick up garbage on my street").

Figure 4.2, "Content Inherent in Children's Block-Building Activity," highlights the possibilities of children's use of content ideas and academic skills as they use their skills of inquiry at each block-building stage. This chart draws

PHOTO 4.8

PHOTO 4.9

FIGURE 4.2. Content Inherent in Children's Block-Building Activity

Key Content Ideas and Vocabulary Examples (Adjectives)	*Skills of Inquiry and Vocabulary Examples (Verbs)*
STAGE I: COLLECTS AND PILES *Science Content: Properties of Matter*	
Physical properties of blocks vary: *Attributes:* • identical • similar *Shape:* • rectangular • cylindrical • triangular • rounded/flat surfaces *Measurement:* • larger-smaller • heavier-lighter • longer/shorter • 6-sided	Comparing and Contrasting leads to sorting of identical, similar, or related properties. • noticing • touching • sorting • grouping • stacking • measuring • lifting • counting
STAGE II: MAKES HORIZONTAL AND VERTICAL ROWS *Science Content: Balance and Stability*	
Balance and stability of a structure is influenced by: 1. placement and position of different-sized and -shaped blocks 2. floor surface	*Using materials in investigation* leads to the discovery of the relationship of size, placement, and position on balance and stability. *Repeated experimentation* leads to generalizations and accuracy in predictions. • placing • lining up • balancing • tumbling
Math: • equivalent length • in ratio of length 1-2, 2-4 • weight • corners • edges • surfaces/faces *Science:* • gravity • stability • balance • linear • horizontal • vertical	

Key Content Ideas and Vocabulary Examples (Adjectives)	Skills of Inquiry and Vocabulary Examples (Verbs)
STAGES III & IV: BRIDGES, ENCLOSURES, AND COMPLEX STRUCTURES *Science & Social Studies Content: Architectural Features*	
Structures vary in number and size of openings. Interior space of structures can vary in length, width, and height.	Using measurement skills to create openings and enclose space. • figuring out • solving a problem
STAGE V: RE-CREATES FAMILIAR ATTRIBUTES OF THE ENVIRONMENT *Social Studies Content: Environmental Structures, Props for Drama*	
Structures vary in function Physical geography defines the use of land surface in a community. *Examples of Structures:* • homes for people • post office • garden store	Communicating observations, ideas, and understandings through dramatization. Using blocks and block props as tools for transforming images. • family • postal delivery person • gardener
STAGE VI: USES CONSTRUCTIONS AND ACCESSORIES AS PROPS FOR DRAMA *Communication/Literacy and Social Studies: Developing Drama and Taking Roles*	
A common language and adequate vocabulary is necessary for communicating with others. Interaction with others helps to clarify ideas, perceptions, and feelings. The use of pictures, graphic representations, and written language helps in the communication of messages.	Increasing the use of productive and receptive oral language, sharing impressions, clarifying ideas. Utilizing pictures and written text to increase knowledge about structures and increasing the sense of "story" in dramatizations.

a parallel between the key content ideas and related vocabulary in the first column and skills of inquiry in the second column that lead to accessing the content. Teachers are continuously making a choice as to whether to comment about the content—the fact that the two blocks are the same length, or the process—the action of comparing length while placing two blocks side by side. The key content ideas on the chart have been abstracted from the more comprehensive content charts in Appendices A–E. The vocabulary in the chart serves as a reminder of choices for initiating conversation at each level.

EXPANDING THE CONTENT DURING CENTER TIME

As we worked with diverse groups of teachers, we found that the most valuable resources for helping them improve their ability to identify content in action and then launch conversations were knowledge of the stages of block-building, and awareness of the content inherent in children's block-building activity. What they discovered was that they were not fluent in using the strategy of initiating conversation that had direct connections to key content ideas. Tapping into children's thinking based on observation presented a challenge. In addition, they found that it was difficult to come up with the language connected with what they understood about the children's thinking. As a way to address this challenge, they studied photographs and videos of the children as they were engaged with blocks. This led to the generation of many samples of statements related to observations that could be used to initiate conversations rich with content. It is important to note that it is not always possible to pick up on what might be the important elements of a child's actions with blocks. The following are samples of the kinds of entry statements for different content areas related to observations:

Linear measure

Block Building, Stage 2:

"I see that you've made a line of blocks as long as the carpet."

Architectural features and linear measure

Block Building, Stage 4:

"I see you made the yard/pen/enclosure for the horses bigger than the one for the ducks."

"I noticed that you used all the same length blocks to fill up the space on the floor inside your building."

"It looks like the blocks on the perimeter, the outside of your building are all the same length."

Reenacting family and community roles

Block Building, Stage 6:

"I see that the door of your garage is just big enough for the little cars but not the big ones."

As with all learning, fluency in initiating and sustaining content-focused conversations with the children in the block center increases with practice. Teachers found that using this approach unleashed thoughtful discussion as well as extended the block-building effort. They also discovered that as they became more active during block center time by *feeding* children's thinking, it brought about a change in the way in which children responded to their presence in the center. They were surprised at how quickly the children sought to share what they had been doing, problems they had solved, and their plans for continuing. As this change in the interactions took hold, the direction on how to strengthen the content possibilities became much clearer.

SEEDING AND LEADING IN THE BLOCK CENTER

Another route toward expanding content in the block center is to seed the center with more resources, in order to stimulate activity and discussion. Figure 4.3 illustrates the possible outcomes of adding specific categories of props. The first column provides a list of concrete props to enrich constructing activity. The second column identifies typical activities that evolve in the use of the props. Finally, the third column lists the key ideas embedded in the activities, along with the vocabulary that can become a part of the discussions. The seeding of a center with print and graphic materials such as photographs and books in response to an observed interest also serves to expand their images of possibilities for construction.

A third route to bringing new content into the block center is that of *leading* activities in the form of adult suggestions and guidance in trying out new ideas related to ongoing constructions. In the block center, the role of leading may take the form of helping a child increase the stability of the structure by widening the base or relocating it onto a more secure surface.

MOVING WITH CONTENT BEYOND THE BLOCK CENTER

Once momentum is built around a topic in the block center, it often leads to large group curriculum experiences that further the topic or theme. There is a great deal of literature available on how to develop themes in action-

FIGURE 4.3. Block Center Props to Seed the Use of Content

I. Props	II. Typical Activity	III. Key Ideas
Wheeled vehicles that vary in size, shape, color, weight	Constructing and using wheeled vehicles on roadways, bridges, ramps, and in tunnels	Starting force and angle of ramp affects speed, distance and direction *Vocabulary: force, angle, faster-slower, further, ramp, tunnel*
Road signs and other such props as gates	Constructing intersecting roadways	Need for traffic control systems *Vocabulary: vehicle names, street, driveway, road, sidewalks, intersections, traffic control signs*
Airplanes and boats	Constructing airports and water ways	Types of transportation *Vocabulary: airport, runway, passenger plane, cargo plane, ship, tugboat, sailboat, ocean, river*
Construction vehicles	Building construction sites	Types of labor and functions of vehicles *Vocabulary: wrecking crane, bulldozer, dump truck, back hoe, concrete truck*
People figures: • Community service • Families	Building structures for different types of figures	Types of structures in a community *Vocabulary: post office-postal worker, bus-bus driver, home-mother, aunt, grandfather*
Animal figures: • Pets • Farm animals • Zoo animals	Habitats and locales Mothers and babies Drama events	Distinctive attributes of animals Animal habitats *Vocabulary: Horse corral, pig pen, cow barn, dog house*

based programs from which teachers can collect ideas (Fromberg, 1995; Katz & Chard, 2000; Scheinfeld, Haigh, & Scheinfeld, 2008).

An analysis of the potential content that would emerge during a selected set of theme activities serves as a critical step in strengthening content. The types of thematic curriculum activities that expand children's experience and knowledge base, and involve the use of academic skills, ranges from trips and classroom visitors to the use of literature, new materials, and projects. The themes that have the greatest impact on children's content acquisition and skill development are ones in which the children can use the new experiences in a variety of ways in the centers. The balance between acquiring new information in high-interest contexts and using it in a variety of ways

> The balance between acquiring new information in high-interest contexts and using it in a variety of ways, is the critical factor in determining whether children will come to own the knowledge and skills.

is the critical factor in determining whether children will come to own the knowledge and skills.

Photo 4.10 depicts a construction that grew out of a theme on bridges. In response to children's emerging interest in bridges, the teacher implemented a series of group activities over a period of 2 weeks. The activities included examining books that featured bridges, taking a local trip to view and photograph different bridge structures, taking photographs of children's block structures that included bridges, and *seeding* the centers with art materials for re-creating bridge structures.

As two children were completing their construction of a bridge scene that incorporated many emerging ideas about bridges, waterways, and roadways, they invited the teacher to "Look. Look at our bridge." The children explained that the bridge was intended for the cars. When the teacher asked for more detail about the path for the cars, they realized that there was no road on top of the bridge. The children then decided that the blocks on top of the bridge would be the towers. A river would run along one side of the bridge and the road on the other side. In response to the teacher's query about the road signs, one of the builders explained that they were placed there to assure that the cars stopped and didn't run into the bridge.

In these interactions, the teacher chose to tap into the content to which the children were cognitively and emotionally tied rather than other possibilities of patterns, number, and size. As illustrated, their content was more closely aligned with standards in social studies, specifically geography. This conversation helped the children clarify their thinking about the relationship between different elements of the bridge scene and the need for further adaptation.

PHOTO 4.10

SUMMARY

Capitalizing on the content that children bring to their activities in the block center requires our focused attention on identifying content possibilities and selecting from the possibilities before initiating conversation. The initiating comments that invite conversation need to avoid short-answer-dead-end questions that tend to stop action as the child begins to figure out what the adult is seeking. Sharing observations serves to reach out to the child rather than asking the child to reach out to the adult. Once conversation begins, it is likely to flow in a direction sparked by the child's interest and sets the stage for teacher contributions, both immediately and in the future. The steps in the interaction include:

- *feeding* children's collection and organization of facts through conversations as they pursue activities of interest in the center, whether initiated by them or us;
- *seeding* their involvement with materials and peers by the timely addition of materials;
- *leading* curriculum activities in order to introduce new content through experiences and interaction.

In order to strengthen children's learning of content, there needs to be a balance between adult-guided activities to expand experiences and child-guided experiences to translate these experiences into meaningful understandings.

CHAPTER 5

Strengthening Content in the Water and Sand Center

My vision has changed about promoting content about water. There is a lot more content in exploration of water than I had realized.

—teacher reflection

Photo 5.1 brings into focus several areas of content information that children discover over and over again but don't really think about as they "play with water." The first big idea they discover is that water flows downward unless acted upon by another force. They pour and they pour and the water always flows down. If they use a pump dispenser, they are forcing water up the pump passage before it is discharged and moves downward again. They don't really think about this contrast in the movement of the direction of water, but they are sufficiently fascinated with the event to return to it many times. Nor do they make the connection between pumping to draw water upward and using a straw to draw water and other fluids up to their mouth using a sucking force.

Similarly, when children pour water through the funnel, they have the opportunity to notice how the water changes shape as it moves from the

PHOTO 5.1

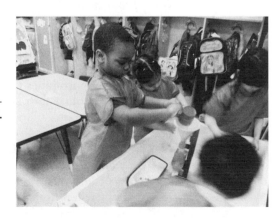

wide opening of the funnel through the narrow passage, although they may not think about it. The big idea here is that water is a fluid material that takes the shape of the container that it is in. It looks different in different shaped containers. When it is flowing out of the funnel it has no shape, and yet when it is in the top segment of the funnel it has a shape that keeps changing, getting smaller.

Clearly, it doesn't make a lot of sense to try to explain these scientific concepts in adult language to prekindergarten and kindergarten children. Nevertheless, they are discovering enough information to pave the road to understanding. That places us in a position to nurture the process through conversations that encourage children to think about the relationship between what they are doing with the materials and what is happening. This means that we need to be familiar with the key content ideas and clear about the developmental stages in the inquiry process.

DEVELOPMENTAL STAGES IN
LEARNING ABOUT WATER AND SAND

The learnings that occur at the water table build on discoveries about the properties of water that occurred during earlier experiences—with bathtub toys, washing hands, jumping in puddles after a rain storm, making mixtures. Prior discoveries about sand emerge the same way, but are more limited due to less exposure.

The identification of developmental stages in children's learning about the properties of water and sand is not as precise and sequential as the stages of block building that were described in Chapter 4. The first stage involves the discovery that water and dry sand have no shape. You can't easily hold either material in your hand and they flow downward. The second stage of discoveries reveals that water and sand exert a force that affects objects. Moving water and sand move objects. When placing objects in water, some of them float—water has a buoyant force. When placing objects on a bed of day sand, they settle a little bit into the sand, displacing some of the sand. At the third stage, children discover a variety of other properties that are unique to each material, depending upon the opportunities presented. For example: Water has surface tension. It holds air bubbles for periods of time. It can be absorbed by other materials. Wet sand retains a shape and can be molded (Chalufour & Worth, 2005; Hill, 1977; Worth & Grollman, 2003). So much of what happens at the water and sand tables result from the fluidity of the material, which allows for so many different kinds of experimentation. After the seemingly endless experiences of filling and emptying containers and pouring from one container to another, the direction of inquiry is usually influenced both by the materials placed in the table and the social setting.

> A well-selected set of materials that narrows the area for discovery is more likely to provoke longer involvement with one type of material and open the door for expanding understandings.

It is important to note that these discoveries are influenced by the way the center is set up. Different categories of materials tend to shape the investigations. There are always containers for picking up and pouring the fluid material. In addition, there are a wide variety of materials that lead to investigating such events using the material as a force to move other objects, as with a water wheel, or floating and sinking, or changing the properties by combining with other materials—coloring the water or wetting the sand. If there are a lot of different kinds of materials at the table, we may see rapid change in the use of materials without a clear focus on experimenting with any of them. A well-selected set of materials that narrows the area for discovery is more likely to provoke longer involvement in experimenting with one kind of event and open the door for teachers to initiate conversation and encourage expansion of children's understandings. In addition, if there are more children than the table can comfortably accommodate, we will see high levels of distractibility as children compete for the resources and space.

EXPANDING THE CONTENT DURING CENTER TIME

When we watch the diversity in children's experimentations, our challenge is to clarify what they are noticing and what sense they are making out of the events they are creating. For example, when alternating the funnels through which they are pouring, or moving the funnels from one container opening to another, are they concerned with size of openings, or just whether the movement of water or sand downward occurs no matter which funnel or container is in use?

When we are observing a child pouring sand onto a turning wheel, as in Photo 5.2, what is the child noticing? Is it the sand going through an opening or a wheel turning, or something else of which we are not aware?

Unless the child spontaneously talks about what is happening, the best we can do is share what we notice in order to invite conversation.

Probably the first piece of information to share in this event would be:

"I noticed that the wheel was turning as you poured the sand."

Depending upon the child's response, the focus can expand to the speed of the turning of the wheel related to the speed of pouring, or the "start-stop" relationship between the pouring action and the wheel turning action.

PHOTO 5.2

> Unless the child spontaneously talks about what is happening, the best we can do is share what we notice in order to invite conversation.

"I wonder if the wheel would turn faster if you poured the sand faster."

Ultimately, whatever seems to be important information to the child is usually validated by the child through repeated experimentation over a period of time. Through the process of exchanging observations and information, content embedded in the activity takes form and can feed the interests of the child to continue collecting more information and using it in different ways. The use of such books as *A Drop of Water* (Wick, 1997) can enrich the conversations between teachers and children as they make connections between the new information they are collecting and their ongoing curriculum experiences.

Figure 5.1 (shown on pp. 66–67) reviews the range of discoveries that children make related to key content ideas that are embedded in the activities at the sand and water table and that result from the fluid nature of the two materials. In the first column, key content ideas are accompanied by additional detail about the beginning foundations for the ideas. In the second column, the performance standard states the key content idea in the form of a child's understanding, and follows with typical behavior indicators that reflect children's use of the content. These behavior indicators alert us to the content children are discovering so that we can develop conversations to strengthen that content, as well as their inquiry skills for investigating the relationship between objects, actions, and events. For example, when the teacher observes the child slowing down the pouring action as the container fills up (Key content idea #1 in Figure 5.1), an entry statement might be:

> Through the process of exchanging observations and information, content embedded in the activity takes form and can feed the interests of the child to continue collecting more information and using it in different ways.

> **The functions of the conversation are to provide the child with the language to talk about discoveries and to encourage further validation through experimentation.**

"I see you are slowing down the pouring of the water (or sand) as the container fills up. Is that because you don't want it to spill over?"

If the child responds to the context of the statement, then the teacher may pursue the idea that once the container is full, the water/sand will fall over the sides and have no shape until it falls into the pool of water/sand in the table. The functions of the conversation are to provide the child with the language to talk about discoveries and to encourage further validation through experimentation. Follow-up think-alouds or questions may include:

"I wonder if the water/sand will always fall downward when it spills out of the container."

An example of a validating statement used when observing children experimenting with tools that change the direction of the movement of water (Key Content Idea #2 listed in Figure 5.1) is:

"I was watching as you pushed on the pump and the water came up to the top before it came out of the opening of the container and fell downward."

If the child is experimenting at a more advanced level, beginning to connect the speed of pumping with the speed of water movement (Key Content Idea # 3), then a sequenced set of comments might be:

"I noticed that when you were pumping faster, the water seemed to come out faster. Did you notice that too?"

When moving water upward, a baster is a more difficult tool for young children to use than a pump. Direct instruction is often needed to coordinate the action of the child with the action of the water. The teacher may guide the child through the mechanics at first:

"Put the baster in the water. Squeeze the top and watch the water move up. Lift the baster out of the water and then squeeze it again and watch the water fall out."

Once the child makes the connection, then the adult can observe:

"Wow. Look at that. You can make the water move up and then down."

FIGURE 5.1. Water and Sand Center: Content and Standards

Key Content Ideas and Supporting Information	Performance Standards and Behavior Indicators
WATER AND SAND: FLUIDITY AND MOVEMENT	
1. Water and dry sand have no shape of their own.	*Understands that water and dry sand have no shape of their own.*
Although sand is made up of particles that do have a fixed shape, they are so small that collections of dry sand take the shape of the container in which it is placed. When the container can no longer hold additional content, the person pouring has no control over how the materials distribute.	Pours water and dry sand into containers that are different sizes and shapes, to over flowing. With experience, slows down the speed of pouring as the container fills up so the material does not overflow.
2. Water and dry sand flow downward unless a force is used to change the direction.	*Understands that water and dry sand move downward unless some action is used to change the direction of movement.*
A force may be applied directly to move sand and water upward by *sucking up* air in the passageway (e.g., pump or baster). A force may be applied indirectly by redirecting a path to point upward and using a force to start the movement of the water or sand through the path, i.e. tubing. Moving air is a force that can be applied to move sand and water horizontally along a surface. The greater the force, the faster the movement.	Experiments with changing the direction of movement of water and dry sand by such action as pushing and using tools such as a straw and a baster. Deliberately changes the direction of movement of water and dry sand.
3. The speed of movement of water and dry sand varies depending upon the size of the path through which it moves and the nature and direction of the force.	*Understands that the speed of movement of water and dry sand varies depending upon the size of the path, and the intensity and direction of the force.*
	Compares and contrasts the speed of movement of water or dry sand as it moves through different sized paths or channels.
	Seeks to control speed by using different sized pouring containers and funnels or changing the speed of the force when using a pump.

Key Content Ideas and Supporting Information	Performance Standards and Behavior Indicators
4. *Moving water or sand is a force that moves other objects.*	*Understands that moving water and dry sand can move other objects.* Experiments with movement of water and sand as a force to move objects, such as a waterwheel.
5. *Water and sand change some of their physical properties when mixed together.*	*Understands that when water and sand mix, some of the physical properties of both materials change.* Investigates and talks about texture of wet and dry sand when molding wet sand. Experiments with adding water to dry sand to change the texture. Experiments with adding sand to water and notices changes in the way the water and sand look.
6. *There are tools for measuring volume of water and sand.*	*Understands that there are tools that can be used to measure volume.* Investigates and compares capacity/volume using such tools as a measuring spoon or cup, quart container.

Teachers found that their experiences in working at strengthening content at the sand and water table were similar to that of the experiences they had with strengthening content in the block center. The task of generating entry and follow-up statements on the spot was not as easy as they thought it would be, partly because they did not feel fluent with the range of content ideas that connected to the actions. Planning possible entry statements in advance helped develop a level of comfort with the approach, allowing teachers to select from possibilities and adjust the dialogue based on the children's responses. As experience increased, it was easier to promote thinking about and testing ideas the children seemed to be generating. Facility in initiating and sustaining conversations in the sand and water center grew out of the study of the key content and standards listed in Figure 5.1. The items on this list are directly connected to the content charts in Appendix A, "Physical Science." The task of developing fluency with the content about water and sand continued to amaze the teachers because they really thought they already knew it.

They realized that in the past they had not been using much of their accumulated content information as they interacted with the children.

> The task of developing fluency with the content of water and sand continued to amaze the teachers because they really thought they already knew it.

STRUCTURED LEARNING OPPORTUNITIES

In addition to *feeding* children's learning with conversations about their expressed interests in the sand and water center, introducing teacher-shaped learning opportunities can lead to the strengthening of content and addressing the standards. The following vignettes illustrate possibilities. The first vignette used the seeding strategy, of introducing a selected set of materials to provoke inquiry. The materials stimulated the discovery of information leading to an increased understanding about the fluidity of water. The second vignette describes a structured activity that took place in a separate area of the classroom and dealt with the idea that water takes the shape of the container that it is in. The third vignette illustrates the kind of conversation that can stimulate children's thinking about buoyancy, another property of water, which is detailed in the water content chart in Appendix A. The fourth vignette focuses on discovering the fact that sand loses fluidity when water is added. The fifth vignette deals with the idea that moving air moves water and that water has surface tension. The sixth and final vignette deals with a key content idea about mixtures, also detailed in the chart in Appendix A.

Vignette # 1

Key Content Idea: Water is a fluid material that has no shape of its own.

In group time, the teacher showed the children four different objects that were being added to the water table. They included a colander, slotted spoon, fishnet, and strainer. She elicited from the children their experiences with the tools. Then she invited them to wonder and share their thoughts about what might happen if you poured water into the different objects. Finally, she advised them that the objects would be in the water table so that they could experiment with them.

At the water table two children engaged in a broad series of typical "water play" activities. They poured water back and forth from various containers and then began experimenting with the new materials. They repeatedly tried to collect water with the fishnet, the slotted spoon, and the colander. They proceeded to silently test the results of pouring water through the new materials. Ultimately, one child brought drama into her activity by placing the colander in the water and declaring

"I made soup."

The teacher who was nearby responded by inquiring whether she could have a taste. When the child lifted the colander up for the teacher to have a taste, there was no soup in the colander.

The question that the teacher asked focused on what happened to the soup. The child immediately put the colander into the water and pointed to it. The teacher summarized the event:

> *"I see the soup now. I think that when you picked up the colander, the soup must have fallen out through the holes. What do you think?"*

After the teacher left, the child tested the idea several times. In the meantime, the teacher returned with several different colored small wooden blocks and put them in the water with the comment,

> *"Here are some vegetables for your soup."*

The child immediately used them, declaring,

> *"I'm making vegetable soup. It's ready."*

Once again the child picked the colander up and the water ran out. The teacher responded,

> *"What happened to the liquid? I can only see the vegetables."*

The child tried several more times to pick up the water and the liquid kept coming through the holes in the colander. The teacher pushed the query further with a think-aloud.

> *"I wonder how you can get vegetables and soup together."*

After several more attempts, the child poured the soup into a jar and told the teacher,

> *"I have your soup ready."*

While tasting the soup, the teacher commented,

> *"I see that you moved the soup to a container that did not have holes like the colander and now the liquid stays in."*

In this event, the child solved the problem. However, it is likely that the child needs more experience with and conversation about these phenomena before she can make a generalization about the connection between water as a fluid and the kind of container needed to hold it.

Vignette # 2

Key Content Idea: Water is a fluid that takes the shape of the container it is in.

The following is a teacher's brief report of an experience in which she introduced a new activity focusing on the fluidity of water. Her goal was to encourage the children to develop an awareness that water takes the shape of the container in which it is placed by pouring water from a container of one shape to one of a different shape. Two children were invited to begin the activity at a table in the water center area. The supplies at the table included containers of different sizes and shapes, a supply source for water, pouring jars and funnels, and colored water the teacher had made with the children. The two children began pouring the colored water into the different shaped containers with little conversation between them. The first observation came from Jacob (who does not appear in Photo 5.3).

Jacob declared: "My water is tall" as he pointed to the cylinder he had just filled. After further experimenting, he requested a container by its shape: "Gimme the square."

The *Teacher* commented: "I noticed when you poured the water in this container it looked like a square."

Maria chimed in: "Mine has a **circle** water on top." Pointing to the pail. The activity and conversation about the shape of water increased as the children began to use the language supplied by the teacher to share their observations.

Maria: Pours more water into the container in front of her and declares "I can make a rectangle."

Teacher: "I wonder how you keep changing the shape of the water."

Maria: "You have to use a rectangle and the water is a rectangle." She points to the bowl on the other side of the table and says, "That one makes a circle."

Teacher (to Jacob): "Do you think you can keep it a square?"

Jacob (with laughter): "Noooo. It changes."

Teacher: "How can we make it stay a square?"

Maria: "We can make it an ice cube."

Jacob: "Put it in the freezer."

Teacher: "Can we make it stay a square on the table?"

Both children chime in: "No it keeps changing."

Jacob: "If you want to change the shape you have to change the container."

PHOTO 5.3

In this event, the teacher introduced the idea of looking at the shape of the water, which was immediately pursued by the children. She did not need to ask them about the shape of the water because they were already talking about it. Because the two children responded so quickly to the idea of discovering *the shape of the water,* she encouraged them to think about what needs to be done to change the shape of water, and whether water will hold the same shape irrespective of the shape of the container that it is in.

As she thought about this experience, the teacher realized that this initial activity sparked a change in children's use of shape words. They began to call each other's attention to the shape of their water, and talked about changing the shape. As more of the class had the opportunity to work with the materials, the children began to talk about the shape of water in other places in the classroom.

After this experience, the teacher reflected that she never would have considered this an important curriculum activity until the content idea of water taking the shape of its container was discussed with a group of colleagues. Further, she realized that the selection of materials was critical for stimulating children to focus on selected events. In her assessment of the success of the activity, she felt that coloring the water, choosing a limited variety of containers, and limiting the size of the group were critical factors.

Vignette # 3

Key Content Idea: Water has a buoyant property. Some objects float in water, others sink.

Children's fascination with the buoyant properties of water begins early and lasts for many years. They tend to focus solely on the object and its behavior without thinking about the properties of the water in the event. In floating and sinking experiments, once they discover that some objects sink and others float, they can begin to change the force of the downward push. This can be done by changing the mass, adding or deleting some material, stacking two materials—one that floats and one that sinks—or changing the shape of the object. In the view of young children, the effect of changing the shape of the object to make it more or less buoyant is more magical than that of adding or reducing the weight. However, the action of changing the shape is actually quite similar to experimenting with a scarf, dropping it when it is open and floats down and then when it is tied in a ball and drops directly to the ground. In this vignette, the teacher described what happened when she targeted the idea that some objects that sink can be made to float.

While initially experimenting with various objects to determine what would sink or float, Jose said to me,

"I think all the big things will float."

I encouraged him to continue using more objects to determine if his prediction was accurate. He took a large rock and it sank. He then shared his observation.

"Some big things and little things float and sink."

Since I had seen Jose struggle with this idea several times during the past few weeks, I decided to challenge him to now think about whether he could change the outcome. So I repeated his change of mind and then posed a problem.

"I see you changed your mind about all big things float. I wonder if you can get the rock to float."

Jose tried several times, and then declared,

"It keeps sinking."

At this point I introduced a new possibility.

"I see. There's a big block and cube floating. Can you use any of these to help you solve the problem?"

I left him to experiment on his own.

The child looked at the materials for a little while, and then tentatively put the rock on top of the big block. He smiled and watched. He repeated this action several times. Several minutes later he called me over and said,

"I did it."

I responded,

> *"I see you put the rock that always sinks on the block that floats and now the block is carrying the rock so it doesn't sink."*

Jose looked at me and said,

> *"Yeah!"*

As I left him to continue experimenting, he proceeded to take other items that sank and put them on the floating block. After that he sorted the objects into "sink" and "float" groups.

The teacher was excited by the child's ability to make use of the information she gave him to solve a problem. As a next step, she planned on offering the children different sized and shaped boats that were also made of different materials. She also gave them flexible materials such as Play-Doh for changing buoyancy by shaping and reshaping the material.

Vignette # 4

Key Content Idea: Water changes the physical properties of sand.

Children quickly discover that wet sand behaves differently than dry sand. Photo 5.4 shows a child discovering that you can't pour wet sand. A teacher observational statement that brings comparison between wet and dry sand to the conversational level can take the form of marveling at what is happening:

> *"Look at that. Wow, that sand is not falling out of the strainer. It just stays there. I bet that wouldn't happen if it was dry sand. What do you think?"*

PHOTO 5.4

As a child then uses her hands to transfer wet sand from the container to the table, another comment that brings this change in the property of the sand to the conversational level might be,

"I was noticing how the sand is sticking to your hands as you take it out of the container."

If the child responds verbally or by shaking his or her hands, a follow-up comment to highlight the difference between dry sand and wet sand might be,

"When you were using the dry sand yesterday, I don't remember that it stuck to your hand this way. Do you remember?"

From this point the interchange can include more comparisons between dry sand and wet sand, and the differences in what you can do with the sand when it behaves like a fluid and when it doesn't. Vocabulary expansion is bedded in this interaction with the contextual use of texture words such as *sticky* and *loose* and action words such as *shaping, molding,* and *pouring.*

Once again, the function of these initial teacher comments is to provoke children to compare and contrast and organize the information they are collecting in ways they can use it in other events with fluid and non-fluid materials.

Teacher-sponsored activities, like the following one, which involves moving beads of water by blowing through a straw, offer a different kind of discovery opportunity.

Vignette # 5

Key Content Ideas: (1) Water has surface tension. It beads up. (2) Moving air is a force that moves objects.

The teacher invited four kindergarten children to experiment with water and straws. She gave each child a straw and asked them to blow through the straw and use their hand to feel the air as it comes out the other end. She encouraged them to experiment, to blow harder and not so hard and then feel the difference. After she placed drops of water on a piece of wax paper in front of each child, she again invited them to blow through the straw, this time to move the drops of water (see Photo 5.5). The children were immediately excited by the results.

"Look. Look. It's moving."

"Now it is moving faster."

PHOTO 5.5

"My drop ran away."

After observing the children and listening for a while the teacher began to share her observations:

> *"Everybody is making the drops move by blowing through the straw. Some drops are moving very fast and some are moving more slowly. How did you make that happen?"*

They talked about blowing harder and softer and drew one another's attention to what they were causing to happen. The teacher was able to reflect that what they were saying was that the harder they blew on the straw, the faster the drops moved. She encouraged them to see how much they could control the speed, how slowly they could make a drop move, and then get it to go faster and faster. One youngster began to test whether she could also make the drops move by blowing without the straw. The idea that moving air is a force that moves objects was not new in their experience, but for most of the children it was not formalized to the point that they could develop a dialogue about the relationship between force, speed, and distance. See the section in Appendix A entitled "Physical Laws of Motion" for the full set of content ideas and behavior indicators.

With continued experimentation, one of the children expressed surprise when two drops joined:

> *"Hey. Where did it go? My drop disappeared."*

At this stage of their investigation, the teacher chose to encourage the child to identify where the drop was when it disappeared, and to experiment in the same way with other drops. She decided that it was too soon to focus their attention on the idea that water has surface tension, which explains why two drops can join and the newly formed larger drop still beads up, like it has a skin holding it together.

Vignette # 6

Key Content Idea: When objects dissolve in water, the physical properties of both the water and the object change.

In the following vignette, the teacher used observation notes to identify a child's emerging understanding of the interaction that occurs when discovering the results of mixing materials. The assessment information not only informs decisions about a focus for initiating and extending conversation, but also for planning additional experiences.

Observation notes: Brett (see Photo 5.6)
- involved in creating mixtures at a table set up for experimenting with mixtures
- pours blue water into yellow water, stirs, and comments, "Look, I made green."
- puts a spoonful of oil into a different cup of water, stirs it: the oil appears to dissolve and then surfaces and reforms into a layer at the surface; comments, "Look the oil came to the top."
- puts a spoonful of salt into a cup of water, stirs it. As salt dissolves and the water becomes a little cloudy, he comments, "Look, it disappeared."
- puts a spoonful of sand into another cup of water, stirs it, and declares, "Look it all went to the bottom, I can still see it."

PHOTO 5.6

- puts a spoonful of colored sprinkles into another cup of water and stirs it. No comment as the sprinkles float on the top of the water then begin to sink.
- leaves the center for a few minutes; upon returning, he notices a change: "Look, I made the water turn pink and blue."

An analysis of this observation reveals that Brett has discovered that when some materials mix with water they disappear. Others do not. The facts he has collected are: (1) when mixing two different colors of water a new color appears, (2) when placing oil in water they don't mix, (3) salt disappears, while sand merely sinks to the bottom without disappearing, and (4) the sprinkles initially float, then partially disappear, changing the color of the water. At this point, he has collected a range of information about dissolving. He has yet to understand the key content idea that "when materials dissolve in water the properties of both the dissolving material and the water change." For additional key ideas in this area, see the section in Appendix A entitled "Matter."

In a follow-up conversation, the teacher chose to focus on comparing and contrasting the differences in the various mixtures, specifically, what was happening to the material that was added to the water. She selected another material at the table—the sugar—and wondered how it would behave when mixed with water. Brett equated sugar to salt and predicted it would disappear. Brett spotted the pebbles and predicted that they would behave like the sand—sink but not dissolve. This teacher reported that she was thinking of expanding the mixtures experiences by initiating a non-heat cooking activities because it would be safe to taste the mixtures and discover that taste is also a change that occurs when some materials are mixed.

SUMMARY

The fluidity of sand and water capture and sustain young children's attention for long periods of time. It is this very fascination with manipulating the materials that opens the door for teachers to strengthen the focus on the content they are uncovering. Observation of their actions and listening to their conversations with peers provides the needed information for initiating conversation and designing additional activities to advance their investigation of the properties of these fluid materials. Conversations with children about what they are noticing as they pour and mix and shape the materials, supports their ongoing collection of information and the construction of understandings about how to control shape and movement of these fluid materials, and events in which they are involved.

CHAPTER 6

Strengthening Content in the Manipulatives Center

A 2-year-old sitting in a high chair spills his Cheerios out of the bowl, returns them to the bowl, one by one, only to spill them out again.

A 4-year-old takes apart and reassembles geosticks a number of times, proudly displays a structure, and then repeats the action of disassembling and assembling.

A 5-year-old stacks small blocks one on top of the other until they tumble, and then starts over again.

What is unique about the "manipulatives center" in a preprimary classroom is that children's particular actions with a material tends to be repeated many times. Something about the material captures a child's interest and drives persistent repetition. Their interest propels them to discover the properties of materials and practice many skills while using them. The 2-year-old described above is developing fine motor coordination through practice while developing a sense of changing quantity by moving cereal pieces from one place to another. The 4-year-old is finding out how to assemble the geosticks, discovering what kinds of shapes appear in the process. The 5-year-old is developing motor coordination in stacking one block on top of the next, and finding out about height and balance. The rich variety of materials in the manipulatives center provides many kinds of opportunities for children to discover object properties and practice skills, and for the adults to feed their learning and foster skill development.

CATEGORIES OF MANIPULATIVE MATERIALS

Essentially there are three types of manipulative materials, each of which has specific purposes. The first type, which we call single-purpose manipulatives, are designed to be used in only one particular way. Examples of single-purpose manipulatives include wooden puzzles and graduated stacking objects. The user is challenged to figure out how the pieces fit together and there is usually only one correct answer. The second type we call sorting and patterning collections. They are designed so that the user makes the choice of how to organize the materials. Typical materials in this group are attribute blocks and assorted collections of different sized miniature animals, people, and objects. The third type we call construction materials. They give the user the widest latitude regarding what to create with the items. Manipulative materials included in this group are interlocking block sets and collections of small varied shaped blocks that are usually intended for use at a table. Both the patterning and construction type materials invite the user to create, organize, and reorganize sets, and build structures.

This broad range of materials housed in the manipulatives center accounts for the fact that the kinds of activity initiated by the children involve different levels of knowledge, skills, and interests. At any given time, one child may be independently using a material of one type at a table alongside another child who is using a material of a different type without interaction between the two. In some instances, the amount of activity may create a distraction for the participants. If it does, there is a need to revisit the decision about the number and type of materials available at any one time in terms of children's ability to focus as they use the materials in increasingly more purposeful ways.

As we think about the materials children choose and observe the different ways in which they might use the same material, it becomes clear that the potentials and limits for children's learning vary according to their interests, the prior knowledge they have accumulated through experience, and the skills they have developed in manipulating the materials. When assembling single-purpose materials, such as the wooden puzzles, success in the task depends upon a child's ability to figure out the relationship between the items to be assembled. That is why the materials in this group type usually include a range in level of difficulty, so the children can become increasingly empowered with successively more complex tasks, such as increasing the number of pieces in the puzzle to make it more difficult to assemble. In contrast, the use of the more open-ended sorting, patterning, and constructing materials gives freer rein to exploring content possibilities. When children pursue their interests, we are in a good position to build on these interests as they become increasingly involved in more difficult tasks with the same materials.

In summary, there is no consistent focus to children's use of the materials we call manipulatives. Therefore, the information gleaned from observing a child is critical to making a decision on what content to feed.

USING MATERIALS
IN DIFFERENT WAYS

It is within the very limits of these manipulative materials that the curriculum potential lies. Photo 6.1 exemplifies the range of children's use of the same material. In this picture we see two children who have created two different stacks of interlocking blocks. One child created consistent color patterns on his two stacks. The other child was more interested in making stacks, irrespective of the color sequence.

As they were sharing their products, they became involved in making length comparisons. In terms of mathematics content, these two children were demonstrating understandings in several different areas: sorting, as they collected the colors they wanted, patterning, as they made the stacks, and the use of baseline for linear measurement. Teacher follow-up to this event might focus on strengthening measurement skills and understandings by engaging in conversation about what they are finding out as they measure. This could be followed up later by the introduction of other kinds of measurement activities related to a class project or individual activity.

As in all centers, the challenge for us is to pick up on the clues the children give us in order to increase their involvement as they use the materials in cognitively stimulating ways and add to their ability to talk about their actions and ideas.

PHOTO 6.1

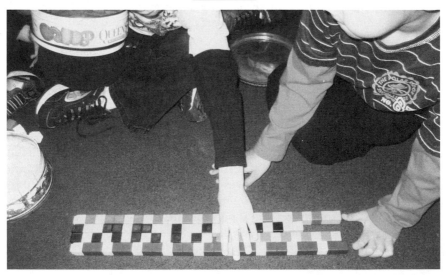

PROGRESSION IN LEVELS
OF USE OF MATERIALS

As discussed in an earlier chapter, children use materials at three different levels. Initially, at the discovery level, they examine and handle them to find out possibilities for use. For example, Lego blocks stay connected when put together in a particular way, but not in all ways. After discovery, the practice level serves as a period of repeated trials during which they confirm their discoveries and develop the motor skills involved in using the material, for example, making and taking apart Lego structures again and again. Finally application level takes form in purposeful use of the materials as exemplified in the construction of castles and other structures with Legos involving drama (Schwartz, 2005).

Throughout the sequence from discovery of possibilities to application, the materials activate the use of the cognitive processing skills we summarized in Chapter 2. These include observing and investigating to discover, comparing and contrasting to verify and organize discoveries, and developing generalizations for application in diverse contexts. Communicating observations, ideas, and understandings, which is almost always listed as one of the cognitive processing skills, may or may not be activated as children manipulate materials. Consequently, one of our goals is to activate this skill in order to capitalize on the potential to develop oral language skills through exchanging perceptions and ideas.

Since the opportunities for strengthening content learning are governed by the level of use of the materials and the nature of the activity, teacher observation serves as the vehicle to track content in use and choose an entry statement to validate and extend the content. When children are discovering and confirming the properties of the material, the *feeding* role is the most likely one to pursue. As discussed in prior chapters, this role follows the format of verbally validating observed use of cognitive skills and talking about content the child may have been discovering, for example, "I noticed that you put two triangle-shaped attribute blocks together and now you have a square." At the practice level, the possibility of *leading* by encouraging variations of action may also occur, such as inviting the child to find out if a square is always created when putting two triangle-shaped blocks together, "I wonder if you would get a square if you took two triangle-shaped blocks in the block center and put them together." As children show that they are applying the newly acquired understandings in different contexts, the teacher's role can include *seeding* the supply of materials for use in different centers of the room. After children begin to discover what happens when triangles in the attribute block collection are joined, the addition of precut triangles and non-squared and squared-rectangles at the collage table can expand opportunities for further discovery and application (Clements, 1999; Schwartz, 2005). Children's selective use of the manipulative materials at different levels leads to differentiated learning and influences the teacher's choice of how to support content learning in process and expand that learning.

CONTENT INHERENT
IN THE USE OF SINGLE-PURPOSE MATERIALS

Puzzles and collections of items that are designed to be organized in serial order by size or other criteria are typical examples of single-purpose materials. The mathematics content that surfaces when children match a puzzle piece to its designated space deals with size, shape, one-to-one matching, and object orientation (see Photo 6.2).

PHOTO 6.2

When children stack graduated cylinders, they are dealing with size order. Speed and accuracy in using these materials increases with practice. The teacher contribution to bringing intuitive knowledge to the conscious level in the use of these materials takes the form of validating the child's problem-solving actions as well as content in use, as in the following comment by a teacher: "I noticed that you kept turning the puzzle piece around before you put it in and it just fit without needing to be turned anymore." In this example, the emphasis is primarily on cognitive processing in order to increase a child's awareness of the thinking involved in accomplishing the task.

CONTENT INHERENT IN THE USE OF SORTING AND PATTERNING MATERIALS

Attribute blocks, beads, links, and miniature vehicles or animals are typical of the materials in this category. The mathematics content that is intuitively used as children sort and pattern these materials based on size, shape, color, and/or class membership involves the use of (1) numbers, in making quantitative comparisons; (2) algebra, in creating patterns; (3) shape geometry, in sorting by shape or using shapes in the pattern unit; (4) locational geometry, in placement of items being organized; and (5) measurement, in figuring out the length of linear patterns. As conversation about the sorted groups and patterns occurs, the vocabulary that goes with this mathematical content serves as a vehicle for further conversation and the extension of skills and understandings.

Sorting and Classifying

An understanding of the progression from simple sorting to higher levels of classification equips the adult to engage in the kinds of conversation and planned activities that expand content learning. The predictable route for thinking about sorting that is detailed in Figure 6.1 begins in toddlerhood with clustering. When the child begins to notice similarities and differences in objects, choices for grouping are possible. The beginnings of classification thinking appear when children show an increased awareness of ways to group and regroup. It is at this time that the teacher can encourage further thinking about ways to sort and classify through invitations to find other criteria for regrouping. The level of sorting behavior from simple to complex is listed in the first column of Figure 6.1. Content possibilities for teacher talk at the different levels of development, leading to classification thinking, are described in the second column.

FIGURE 6.1. Progression Leading to Classification.

Level	Content possibilities for teacher-talk
Clustering: based on personal experiences rather than the objective properties	Limited unless the child declares the reason for grouping the objects, e.g., "my toys"
Simple pairing to exhaustive sorting based on physical properties	Labeling of the identical properties, e.g., two red triangles, same size, all the red triangles that are the same size
Classification, Stage 1 Grouping including two variables, e.g., red and blue triangles in one group and yellow and green triangles in the other group	Comparing and contrasting two groups in terms of variable in common (all triangles), and the variable that is distinct (different colors)
Classification, Stage 2 Grouping based on class membership, e.g., land, water, or airborne vehicles; or function, e.g., woodworking or cooking tools	Identifying the classification criteria Analyzing the similarities and differences in the groups

Source: Abstracted from Good, 1977.

In Photo 6.3 we see the results of a child's response to an invitation to reorder a set that was initially sorted by color. When the adult commented on the color sort, "I see you have sorted the bears by color. I wonder if there is another way you can sort them," the child proceeded to pattern each color group in single alternation by size. In the subsequent interaction, she pointed out to the adult her sequence of the items—big, little, big, little—without speaking. The adult verbalized, "Oh, now you have placed the bears in a pattern of big-little, big-little, big-little." The child nodded in agreement.

PHOTO 6.3

The ability to classify is progressive, becoming increasingly more complex over the years. It is not a question of whether young children can classify, but rather where they are on the spectrum from simple sorting based on physical properties to sophisticated classification that rests solely on the understanding of the relationship between objects in groups (e.g., all the farm animals), and between actions and outcomes (e.g., heating melts frozen materials).

Patterning

Strengthening content in the area of patterning requires increasing recognition of the levels of complexity of patterning from single alternation (AB), to double alternation (AABB), to two-one (ABB), and on to longer pattern units. There is a difference between labeling items in a pattern sequence and being consciously aware of the repeated pattern unit. Over the years as we worked with teachers, we found that they responded to children's patterning products by engaging with a child in naming all the items in the sequence of their pattern. They did not think about labeling the pattern unit. After they introduced the idea of naming the pattern unit using such statements as:

"If I were to give your pattern a name, I would call it a triangle-circle pattern. What do you think of that as a name for your pattern?"

they discovered that the children were spontaneously talking about their patterns with peers and adult, giving them pattern titles.

CONTENT INHERENT
IN THE USE OF CONSTRUCTION MATERIALS

Construction materials include building and interlocking materials, such as table blocks and Legos. For consideration of developmental levels in using the small wooden and plastic blocks and points of entry to strengthen content learning and skill development, we refer the reader to Chapter 4, "Strengthening Content in the Block Center." The interlocking blocks open up more possibilities for children to re-create familiar objects in their environment. Once children discover the possibilities for use of the materials, they will engage in a variety of more complex construction activities, often ending in drama. The child in Photo 6.4 is in the midst of making a pair of construction vehicles that may then be used in a drama activity. When the use of manipulatives become props for drama, teacher-child conversations are likely to follow different paths.

PHOTO 6.4

ROLE OF THE TEACHER

In the manipulatives area the teacher can take on all three roles described in Chapter 3, namely *seeding, feeding,* and *leading.* Materials are deliberately placed or "seeded" in the center to activate the use of specific content and skills. Talking with children about observations of their actions fulfills the *feeding* role. *Leading* takes the form of providing instruction on ways to use the materials and implementing focused group activities that extend children's interests in pursuing content ideas and developing skills.

Since many of the manipulatives have a range in which their use can become more and more complex, as discussed earlier, the decision of how to feed children's thinking rests in an assessment of what content and skills are being used and at what level. Take, for example, the following list of the levels of use of attribute blocks when organizing them to fit into a picture (Clements, 1999).

- Level 1–matching a block shape to individual outlines of shapes
- Level 2–finding and matching shapes within a picture made up of different shapes
- Level 3–organizing shapes to fill in an outlined space

Identification of the level of activity guides the entry for conversation. At Level 1, content conversation is most likely to feature the number of sides of a shape that exactly matches the picture of the shape. A teacher might say:

"I noticed that when you put the hexagon on the picture of the parallelogram, it didn't match on all sides and you took it off. Then you found the picture of the hexagon, and when you put the block back on top of it, all six sides matched."

Level 2 offers more options for validating content due to the fact that children will use different strategies to recreate the picture. The teacher comment might be,

> *"I noticed that you held the shape in your hand, looked at the picture, and then decided exactly where to put it. How did you figure that out?"*

Similarly, at Level 3, there are likely to be many options for initiating content conversation, depending upon the observed strategies used by a child. For example,

> *"I noticed that first you placed pieces along the outer edges and then you worked at filling in the middle. Did you find that easier or harder to do than starting at the top and working downward in the puzzle?"*

THE INTERPLAY BETWEEN
ADULT- AND CHILD-DRIVEN ACTIVITIES

The tasks children choose to pursue as they use manipulative materials shape how adults craft the interplay between what the children know and can do, and the adult contributions to expand these understandings through planned group activities. It is important to keep in mind that it is not critical whether a teacher-planned activity or children's involvement in centers sparks the interplay, but rather that the interplay is ongoing.

As discussed above, patterning is a dominant activity in the manipulative center because of the nature of the materials. Once patterning emerges as a strong interest, it can be fed through activities in other centers. The teacher might initiate a project of making decorations for a class party, such as placemats and wall hangings that involve creating and extending patterns. Through these kinds of activities, the children can further explore possibilities for patterning and discover different ways to pursue their interest in different contexts. This kind of involvement may lead to the making of a class reference book with many samples of standard patterns, such as single alternation and double alternation, along with less familiar patterns, such as 1-2-2 (e.g., one red heart, two blue stars, two green stars). When children have the opportunity to use new understandings and skills in diverse activities, they achieve greater and greater mastery of the content ideas and related skills.

The following description of a segment of program activities illustrates what we mean by the interplay between teacher- and child-driven activities that are vested with content. In this set of events, the spark to stimulate interest in creating patterns began with a group activity in which the teacher engaged the children in creating single alternation patterns with a variety of materials.

The interface between the teacher focus on patterning with materials in a group setting and the children's independent pursuit of this idea in different centers is illustrated in the next set of photos taken during center time within the next few days. In Photo 6.5 the child is displaying how she created patterned sequences of colors with dinosaurs in a single-alternation pattern.

Photo 6.6 illustrates a different context for pursuing the patterning idea. Here the child is using wooden blocks to create a pattern based on position of blocks irrespective of the shape. Note that he has placed the blocks in an alternating horizontal and vertical position.

The appearance of patterning activity in the different centers indicates that the teacher stimulus to focus on patterns successfully connected with children's interests, leading them to expand their exploration of possibilities. In instances where children engage in conversations about the way they are organizing the materials they are working with, the door is open for the teacher to extend thinking about patterns.

PHOTO 6.5

PHOTO 6.6

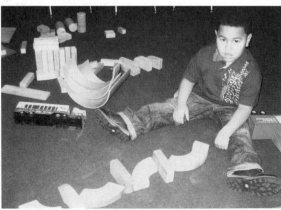

Children's enthusiasm in generating their own color patterns signaled the teacher to keep expanding their experiences to discover other bases for creating patterns, such as shape. The interface between the teacher-planned activities and children's interests continued as she took them on trips to find and record different kinds of patterns in the physical environment, read poems to uncover language patterns, and explored patterns in music. When these additional experiences appeared in children's center activities she was able to engage in conversations that helped children increase their recognition and use of visual, auditory, and language patterns.

CURRICULAR CONNECTIONS

As mentioned earlier, what children bring to their activities with manipulatives shapes what they are likely to do with them. They are continually making connections with prior non-school experiences as well as with school experiences. The following is a typical example of the way in which a series of teacher-initiated activities on a topic translated into children's use of manipulative materials. The teacher had developed the topic of animals and their characteristics over a period of a couple of weeks, using books, photographs, and miniature rubber and plastic animals in order to help children collect and organize information. The following event took place with miniature zoo and jungle animals that had been moved from the manipulative center to the block area.

TOPIC: ANIMALS AND THEIR CHARACTERISTICS

Phase I: Observation Preceding Interaction

In the block area, two boys were using small hard rubber zoo animals in drama events of their own design. One boy was "feeding" a small fox to a rhinoceros, declaring "Look! He's eating it." The child repeated the action and the comments several times.

A short while later, he carried an adult rubber elephant over to the teacher who was sitting at the Play-Doh table nearby, once again requesting attention to his activity. He exclaimed, "Look! An elephant."

The children at the Play-Doh table were using different objects to make stamp patterns in the playdough. He picked up on this action, taking some playdough, flattening it, and making an elephant footprint.

Child: "Look. Look. I made it."

Phase II: Conversation and Follow-Up Actions

Teacher: "Yes. I see, you made a footprint with the elephant's foot."

The child returned to the block area with the playdough footprint and showed his product to the classroom visitor.

> *Child:* "Look," as he points to the footprint. Child silently matches the elephant foot to the print.
> *Visitor:* "I see you made a print with the elephant's foot."
> *Child:* "Yeah," and placed the foot of the elephant onto the print in the playdough.
> *Visitor:* "It just fits. I wonder if you made a footprint with the other elephant [pointing to the smaller one] if it would look the same."

The child turns over the playdough and makes a footprint with the smaller elephant. He looks at both sides alternately several times and then comments, "It's bigger," referring to the first print. He proceeds to repeat the footprinting of the large and small elephant and repeatedly matches the elephant feet to the prints that he makes.

The child returns to the teacher and shares with her his new discovery. As he flips the playdough from side to side, he points to the larger prints and says, "Look. It's bigger."

> *Teacher:* [Points to the smaller prints.] "Yes. It looks like you used the small elephant to make these prints."
> *Child:* "Yeah."

While this interaction was taking place, another child in the center who had been silently pairing each large animal with its matching smaller animal took the two giraffes and called the visitor's attention to his observation that the neck of the larger giraffe is longer than that of the smaller one. The visitor validates his observation and the child continues to stroke the necks of the two animals, repeating his statement.

In this interchange, the children led the way to strengthening their understanding of size relationships. The adult role initially was one of describing actions. The first child's response opened the door for encouraging further investigation of the relationship between the object used to make the footprint and the footprint obtained. Provision of language by the adult helped the child to use language to share his discovery. The comment of the second child offers strong support for the idea that when a child is located near another child's learning event, it also stimulates his or her learning.

The teacher reflected on the fact that these two children were focusing on comparative size, although she had discussed with them other animal characteristics over the period of a couple of weeks. The interesting revelation was that we can't necessarily predict which avenue a child will follow in pursuing a teacher-initiated curriculum topic as broad as this one. The important factor here is that adults were able to capture the children's interests and help them become more consciously aware of size comparisons.

SUMMARY

Unlike other center areas, the manipulatives center sparks a wide range of activities, not only within the center area but throughout the room. A great deal of motor-skill development accompanies repeated use of the materials, which involves considerable practice in the skills generally associated with academic content in literacy learning and mathematics. Visual discrimination and construction of shapes, letters, numerals, sorting, and patterns permeate the use of the materials. While these materials rarely spur the development of themes, they often serve as props in pursuing content that is featured in themes. Opportunities for strengthening content and meeting the standards are ever-present as children use these materials.

CHAPTER 7

Strengthening Content in the Drama Center

The purpose of the drama center in preprimary classrooms is to provide an inviting place for young children to re-create their experiences in their own way. This can take the form of stories drawn from their daily lives or ones that include segments of both real and imagined experiences. Whether the roles in the drama that young children take on involve familiar figures, or imagined characters from stories to which they have been exposed through media or other sources, the drama they create meets their needs to explore and clarify their own ideas and feelings, along with that of others included in the drama.

FORMS OF DRAMATIC PLAY

Dramatic play essentially takes two forms: solitary play, in which the child plays alone, and sociodramatic play, which takes place in interaction with others. Sociodramatic play has the potential for fostering the following:

1. Creativity, as children "gather scattered experiences and create out of them a new combination";
2. Intellectual growth, through the process of reconfiguring their own experiences in the light of those of others in the play situation; and
3. Social skills, through interaction with peers (adapted from Smilansky, 1968, p. 12).

What is most interesting about the research findings of Smilansky was the difference in the quality of sociodramatic play of youngsters from different backgrounds. Observations of the behavior patterns of youngsters with less exposure to life's experiences were characterized by repetition with a lack of elaboration. These findings alert us to the importance of enriching the children's lives through focused experiences followed by giving them opportunities to explore the meaning of these experiences in child-directed drama activities.

VIEWS ABOUT ADULT INVOLVEMENT

There are three views about adult involvement with content in the drama center.

- The first and most common approach is to seed the drama center with varied materials and provide maximum freedom for the children to use the materials in their own way with little or no adult involvement. In this approach, teachers may observe the drama, but do not usually engage with the children. Teachers who favor the observer role are concerned that adult involvement may well get in the way of what the child or children are trying to better understand or the feelings that they are trying to work out through their drama. For example, if several children in a drama center set up as a home environment are taking the roles of the authority figures as well as the less powerful individuals in their lives, adult involvement may well get in the way of what they are trying to better understand emotionally. The teachers with this view also feel that it is difficult to find a productive route for conversation when children are involved in their own self-directed drama. Take for example the activity of the children in Photo 7.1. One child is sitting at the edge of the drama center writing a menu for a dinner she plans to serve. When asked by a peer what she was writing, she said "I'm making a dinner." Another child, sitting at the main table, is singing while she dresses her baby. This situation is typical of the kinds of events that teachers do not consider viable for strengthening content.

- A second approach often used in program development is to seed the drama center with materials that replicate a familiar site, such as the doctor's office, to encourage children to engage in drama about their experiences at those sites. This requires considerable teacher involvement in initiating the drama through focused discussions and curriculum experiences with the total group, along with a supply of materials that go with the theme. This approach allows for teacher choice in engaging with children during their dramatizations, either about their understandings of roles related to the social studies content or introducing new content that contributes to the development of key ideas as they pursue their drama.

<u>**PHOTO 7.1**</u>

- A third approach, exemplified in the work of Paley, is to elicit from children the stories they are telling through their drama, and to involve them in retelling the story through repeating the drama with others. Here, the teacher is actively involved in supporting children's ability to create and narrate their own stories by writing them down and rereading them as a way to stimulate their reenacting the story with others (Paley, 1981, 2004, 2010). Paley's extensive research on the effects of nurturing fantasy play on children's social-emotional and literacy development is well described in her publications. For further examination of ways to strengthen literacy through capturing the stories children create in drama we encourage the reader to pursue Paley's work.

In this chapter we focus our discussion on the second approach, strengthening content through shaping drama activities within the context of themes.

ENRICHING CURRICULUM
THROUGH FOCUSED PROGRAM EXPERIENCES

There are a variety of options for designing focused curriculum activities that will spark children's interest in reenacting experiences in the drama center. The strongest possibilities for drama flow from the experiences with which children have already had some exposure, such as shopping, family-life activities such as going on a picnic, observation of the actions of fire and police personnel, travel on different kinds of vehicles, and visits to medical facilities and recreational centers. Sometimes children spark a topic or theme through their spontaneous activities in centers, such as fascination with firefighters or trucks. Other times, the theme is introduced by the teacher. A critical factor for increasing children's knowledge and understandings of content rests in the continuing cycle between exposure to a new theme or topic experiences that are planned by the adult and children's opportunity to develop understandings flowing from those new experiences during center time.

CONTENT FOCUS IN THEME DEVELOPMENT

The thematic approach to curriculum has served as a hallmark of quality programs for young children for decades, beginning with the Dewey era (Dewey, 1963; Dodge & Colker, 1992; Katz & Chard, 2000; Read, 1971; Thompson, 1991; Wien, 2008). The early childhood professional literature is rich with information on how to plan themes, as well as samples of fully developed themes. While sample themes include many activities that are considered developmentally appropriate, they usually give little attention to the identification

> A critical factor for increasing children's knowledge and understandings of content rests in the continuing cycle between exposure to new theme or topic experiences that are planned by the adult and children's opportunity to develop understandings flowing from those new experiences during center time.

of key ideas in the content areas that will permeate the theme activities. Planning familiar themes using key ideas in the content areas serves as a way to focus on the content to be learned and the standards children will need to meet. Similarly, knowing the key ideas also helps teacher plan for developing conversations with the children throughout the theme activities.

This new layer of professional thinking sharpens teachers' observations of how children are building understandings when engaged in center and group activity and reshapes their approach to theme planning. The provision of child-choice time to sort out and make sense of theme experiences, continues to be a vital part of theme development. Only as we observe what impact the new experiences have on children's understandings can we plan further experiences to strengthen emerging knowledge. As indicated in Chapter 3, planning a theme, whether the topic was generated by the teacher or the children, begins with the identification of the key concepts and related vocabulary. It continues with the planning of the launch and follow-up activities for both group and center time and ends with a culminating class experience. This can be facilitated using the theme planning sheet (Figure 3.2). Also a guide for planning and implementing themes appears in Appendix G.

We offer the following description and analysis of one theme as an example of a teacher's adventure in designing developmentally appropriate theme activities that help children make connections with key ideas in the content areas, strengthen their communication skills, and move toward meeting some of the behavior indicators that show children have met local or State learning or performance standards.

SUPERMARKET THEME

The teacher who planned this theme began by thinking about children's prior shopping experiences. She realized that during the children's many visits to the supermarket, they had collected a great deal of information. However, in thinking about the many events that transpire in a supermarket, it would

> Planning familiar themes using key ideas in the content areas serves as a way to focus on the content to be learned and the standards children will need to meet.

be difficult to identify what information they had collected and how they had organized their understanding of these experiences.

She began by thinking about the visible actions that occur in a supermarket, such as collecting food items, paying for the items, packing, and leaving. These actions constitute the essence of the "buyer-seller" enterprise listed under the "Economics" key content ideas in Appendix E. What was not visible to young children was the underlying structure and organization of the market, as well as the series of events that transpired to make the supermarket resources available to consumers. For example, they were not aware of the many steps that occur from the time the food arrives at the store to the placing of the food where shoppers can find it.

Even when children do notice events in the supermarket and talk about them, they do not necessarily make sense to them. Take, for example, the last step at the checkout counter, which deals with the idea of exchange of goods for some kind of payment. This step involves recording the cost of the food items, declaring a total amount due, a payment action, and packing the items. In small, local convenience stores the initial action of recording the cost of each item may take the form of typing on a cash register. In larger markets, the pricing actions involve a search for the bar code, scanning the item and/ or typing in information on some machine. The procedure for paying for the groceries is also difficult for young children to comprehend. Sometimes there is a handing over of money. Other times money is being transferred in both directions. Still at other times, there is no money visible, only a card that is pushed through a machine.

PHASE 1: Identifying Key Content Ideas and Vocabulary

The first step in developing the supermarket theme involved thinking about and making a selection from the key content ideas in the different subject areas that might be embedded in the supermarket theme, as shown in Figure 7.1 (shown on pp. 98–99). The ideas are drawn from economics as well as mathematics, science, and language and literacy. This identification of key ideas helps the teacher recognize which ideas children are already generating. This, in turn, provides opportunities to build on what they already know and are likely to care about. The key ideas the teacher chose to focus on in developing the supermarket theme are listed in Figure 7.1. In the first column of the chart, the key ideas from the four subject areas and how they apply to the supermarket theme are listed. In the second column is a list of behavior indicators that are likely to be observed during theme activities.

Next, a list of theme-related key vocabulary was developed for use in conversations during theme activities. This list spanned a broad range, including supermarket terms such as section labels and job roles, and shoppers' language, such as *purchase, shopping cart,* and *shopping list.* Fluency with these terms allowed the teacher to help children develop the necessary repertoire of words to dramatize roles with peers and talk about their experiences with family, using such terms as *aisle, dairy,* names of vegetables, and *cashier.*

The following description of how the theme unfolded reveals ways in which the focused curriculum activities engaged and sustained children's interest and further developed content knowledge, communication skills, and understandings through action and interaction around key content ideas.

PHASE 2: Launching the Theme

The theme plan was launched at group time with a discussion about children's experiences in a supermarket. As they talked about their recall and impressions, the teacher raised the possibility of setting up the drama center as a supermarket. The children were enthusiastic and a conversation ensued about the resources that would be needed. Requests, along with an explanation, were sent out to the parents to send in clean empty food containers for stocking the store.

Several days later, when the stock was large enough, the teacher posed the question with the class at group time of how to arrange the furniture and stock the shelves in the drama center. Children's ideas about where to place the containers revealed their awareness of ways in which to classify foods and the food storage needs, such as the refrigerator for milk and the shelves for the boxes and cans. When the children went to the center and began to place the containers on shelves, the conversation reverted to sorting based on specific criteria. Those who were involved in the mathematics of size persisted in arranging and rearranging the containers to fit in designated spaces. Others were concerned with grouping the containers based on types of food irrespective of size and shape. The two different sets of views led to a group time conversation about different ways to sort and group the boxes and cans on the shelves. As the setting-up activity in the center continued, the teacher was able to raise such questions as, "How will the buyer know how much an item will cost?" thereby provoking children to think about price labels and paying for goods. Once the procedure of making labels was introduced, some children became interested in making other signs, such as "Open" and "Closed," building their understanding that written language is one form of communication.

PHASE 3: Observation of Children's Initial Activities

The dramatic activities that occurred during the first couple of days took the form of brief spurts of interest in discovering how the supermarket resources work and reenacting roles. Photos 7.2 to 7.5 (shown on p. 99),

FIGURE 7.1. Content Embedded in Supermarket Theme

Key Content Ideas and Performance Standards Related to the Theme	*Behavior Indicators*
SOCIAL STUDIES	
Economics: *Essential functions in an economic community are fulfilled by differentiated job roles.* Recognizes that different jobs in a supermarket require different skills.	Talks about and dramatizes roles and the different kinds of skills required to fulfill those roles in a supermarket.
In an economic community, people provide goods and services in exchange for some form of payment, money or equally valued goods or services. Recognizes that buyers pay sellers for food and other merchandise in the supermarket.	Dramatizes job roles associated with various settings in the supermarket. Demonstrates awareness of the need to make an exchange for objects and service with materials or money.
MATHEMATICS	
Algebra: *Sets are made up of collections of objects, events, or ideas that are created for a reason. Sets can be sorted and grouped based on selected criteria.* Recognizes that, in the supermarket, food and other merchandise are grouped and located based upon membership in a class, e.g. produce, frozen goods, dairy.	Talks about the criteria for organizing food materials in the supermarket and uses selected criteria for grouping food items in the classroom interest center.
Number: *Numerals are written representations of number.* Recognizes that a written number is used to designate cost of an item.	Looks for the cost of an item on the package. Makes price signs for containers in drama center.
Measurement: *Physical properties of objects can be measured and compared using non-standard and/or standard units.* The placement of containers on shelves or in tote bags depends upon the size of the container and the space available.	Places food on shelves in size order, arranges food in shopping cart to fit the area available.
Geometry: *2-D and 3-D shapes have unique properties that distinguish them from one another.* Realizes that the shapes of boxes and containers on the shelves of a supermarket vary.	Locates different packaged foods and talks about the shape cues they use to find them.
Geometry: *Space, location, position, and direction are critical components for understanding spatial relationships.* Realizes that the position and location of items in the supermarket can be identified by written cues and/or verbal descriptions.	Specifies locations and describes spatial relationships of supermarket items, such as next to, over, other side.

Key Content Ideas and Performance Standards Related to the Theme	Behavior Indicators
SCIENCE	
Matter: *Objects have properties that can be described, compared, and changed. Objects can be grouped based on identical or similar properties.* Understands that foods in the supermarket vary in such properties as temperature, size, shape, and texture.	Uses language to describe and compare properties of foods and food containers. Talks about the conditions provided for storing foods, such as freezers, refrigerators, vegetable bins, and open shelves.
LANGUAGE AND LITERACY	
Writing: *Understands the need to use graphic and written forms of recording for different purposes.* Signs in the supermarket provide directions for finding food items. Labels on the food containers provide information of cost.	Makes signs as location markers when setting up a supermarket in the drama center. Looks for signs to help find grocery items in the drama center.

PHOTO 7.2

PHOTO 7.3

PHOTO 7.4

PHOTO 7.5

provide typical illustrations of prekindergarten and kindergarten children's awareness of discrete events that occur, beginning with the discovery of how the cash register works (Photo 7.2). Money was handled by a rotating cast of cashiers reflecting awareness that there is some kind of payment activity at the market. They also engaged in dramatizing typical roles of buyers and sellers (Photo 7.3). Here the child, shopping with her baby, is paying for groceries and the cashier is giving her change.

As the teacher observed children talking to one another about what to buy, she provided grocery flyers and blank shopping lists to encourage the interested children to make selections from the flyers. See Photo 7.4 of the child writing her shopping list and Photo 7.5 of a child using his list to select items from the shelf.

In all of the dramatizations illustrated in the photos, the children were re-creating actions they had observed as a way to better understand them. From the teacher's perspective, the nature of the actions during the dramatizations limited efforts to stimulate conversation that could contribute to a better understanding of the supermarket as an economic enterprise. However, she found that she was able to use the information she gained from observations of the children's work in setting up the center as well as in their dramatizations to plan the next step. This required revisiting the key ideas listed in the content charts in Economics (Appendix E), Mathematics (Appendix D), Science (Appendix A), and Language and Literacy (Appendix F).

The goals of strengthening these understandings through conversations and expanded focused experiences grounded the planning for the next phase in the development of the theme.

PHASE 4: Strengthening Content
Understandings Through Focused Experiences

In order to expand children's emerging understandings of the key content ideas about the supermarket listed in Figure 7.1, the teacher decided to take the children on a visit to the supermarket. She established a purpose for the visit by reading *Pancakes, Pancakes* (Carle, 1990), and then planned with them to buy food materials to make pancakes for a class cooking event. During the planning session, the children shared their expectations of what they would see at the market.

The teacher focused children's attention on the organization of the supermarket by giving each child a card with the picture and label of one needed food item for which they were responsible for finding. Upon arrival at the store, the manager talked with the children about his job. He also pointed out the signs that listed the foods located in each aisle. Except for the meat department, children had the opportunity to observe and talk with department managers about how food arrives at the store and how it is moved from arrival to the shelves.

The teachers and parents accompanied small groups of children as they searched for their assigned food, helping them make connections between the category of food item they were assigned to obtain and labels on the aisles. For example, the child with a photograph and label for *eggs* found the dairy aisle by matching the word on his egg picture with the lists of items on the aisle sign. The child with the picture of pancake syrup asked the adult to read all the aisle signs until he found the one that listed syrups. Once he located the syrup section, he used his picture to find the specific brand.

PHASE 5: Impact on Drama Activities in the Classroom

Upon return to the school, the results of the field trip were reflected in several ways. The teacher observed more complex dramatizations in reenacting roles in the drama center. The children also requested more information about handling money, and for more of the clothing associated with the different roles. The impact on activities in the expressive art center took the form of making additional props, such as hats for department managers.

In addition, the teacher chose to guide more activities. She initiated the idea of making a class trip book so the children could replay their supermarket experience by viewing the photographs and discussing more about what they recalled about the way a supermarket is arranged, and how the different segments work. Based on this experience, the teacher decided that next year she would visit the market more than once with a different focus for each trip to help the children expand on the key content ideas.

TEACHER REFLECTION

The teacher noted that she had taken groups of children to the supermarket a number of times in previous years, but had never realized how much content could be developed until she studied the possibilities in terms of key ideas in the content areas. She marveled at how interested the children were in pursuing the ideas she introduced in the areas of organization of merchandise and the job roles in this economic enterprise. Their actions in the drama center took on new vitality following the trip, as more children participated in reenacting different job roles and the content of the drama became more complex.

Using Figure 7.1 as a guide, the teacher began to think about how to further engage the children in high-interest tasks that serve to focus their attention on selected key ideas. One possibility was to reach out to the home settings, informing the parents about the content focus in the ongoing theme and inviting the parents to report changes they noticed in the actions and conversation of their children when shopping at the supermarket. She also considered such ideas as visiting a different kind of market to look for similarities and differences in the workforce and the job roles and organization of the store items, or inviting a member of the supermarket staff as a class visitor to talk about his or her job role.

What was most important to this teacher was her new understanding about how the consideration of key ideas in the content areas gives focus to the planning of theme activities that conform with the educational values of an action-based learning environment. The use of the theme-planning guide in Appendix G was now viewed in a different light because it included the identification of key content ideas and performance standards that the activities will address. Appendix I includes a completed theme planning guide for the topic of Shoes, as well as guidelines for developing a theme.

SUMMARY

The drama center serves as a place for children to re-create many of their experiences, to better understand the roles and the dynamics of interaction involving people with whom they have had contact. While it is most often organized to nurture drama about home and family life, it offers a rich opportunity to support the development of curriculum themes dealing with everyday events in their lives, such as riding on a bus or novelty experiences such as a trip to a pumpkin farm. Themes offer a rich array of possibilities for feeding the development of key ideas in the content areas as children pursue activities of high interest. The drama center provides the necessary site for children to incorporate the new theme experiences into their existing well of knowledge. Opportunities to translate experiences into their own drama are one of the critical variables for building content understandings. For the teacher, observation of the drama events provides a window into knowing what sense the children are making of the focused theme experiences and how their content knowledge is taking form.

CHAPTER 8

Strengthening Content in the Expressive Arts and Literacy Centers

Art helps us put our life's experiences into symbolic form so we can stand
back, look at it and share it.

—Robert Schirrmacher,
Art and Creative Development for Young Children, p. 4

Strengthening content in the expressive arts and literacy centers addresses two
major goals in early childhood education: (1) to strengthen children's ability
to communicate, and (2) to nurture the creative potential of each individual
child. Children express the many impressions, ideas, feelings, opinions, and
wishes bubbling in their heads not only through language and actions but
also by using the media materials. Whether we are talking about expression
through written and oral language or through the use of expressive art resources, the goal is to strengthen communicative abilities that establish one's
own identity within a social community. Given the fact that young children
can often express themselves more clearly through the use of media materials than they can through written and spoken language, it is important that
we look at strengthening content in these areas side by side.

LITERACY CONTENT

Content and skills in literacy focus on communication through mastery of
the spoken and written language of the culture. There is extensive professional literature on both the content and process of literacy development
during the early childhood years (Beaty & Pratt, 2007; Ollila & Mayfield,
1992). For purposes of the discussion in this chapter about how to strength-
en content, we briefly summarize generally accepted understandings about
literacy.

Listening and speaking abilities mature through multiple opportunities to receive and produce language as a way to communicate in a variety of contexts that meet personal and social needs. Vocabulary expands through multiple experiences of listening to and using language to communicate. Fluency with the rules of the language system grows over time. Increasing discrimination of language sounds—phonemic awareness—expands through exposure to focused experiences. The content target in oral language that leads to effective communication are embraced in these ideas.

The content in reading and writing builds on oral language content. It centers on recognition of the relationship between spoken and written language and the rules for transforming oral language to text form as a means of communication. Strengthening the content and skills in literacy involve extensive amounts of:

1. *Leading* by modeling meaningful use of oral and written language, the provision of experiences to stimulate the use of language for expressive purposes, and guided practice of discrete skills in high-interest contexts,
2. *Feeding* through engaging in authentic conversations directly related to children's involvement in activities and being an attentive listener when children engage in communicative activities,
3. *Seeding* by provision of materials that stimulate and support children's literacy skills in their self-directed activities in centers and projects.

EXPRESSIVE ART CONTENT

Content in the area of expressive art involves communicating through using the multi-media materials. Communication occurs through the use of graphic and plastic art materials—drawing, painting, constructing models, and other products—that represent children's experiences, understandings, feelings, and reactions to personal events. There are two approaches to thinking about content and skills in the expressive arts. One approach includes both the development of skills in using the media materials as well as the use of these skills for personal expression. The other approach limits the view of content to the period when children are sufficiently familiar with the tools to use them purposefully as a means of expression. The teaching role in strengthening content in the expressive arts, therefore, takes a unique form at each level:

1. *Leading:* when children are learning how to use the tools, instruction takes the form of demonstrating and modeling at timely moments in

response to children's interest. After children know how to use the tools, *leading* takes the form of provision of experiences to stimulate the use of media materials for expressive purposes and orchestrating group conversations about children's processes and expressive art products.

2. *Feeding:* engaging children in authentic conversations about their processes and products; being an attentive listener when they choose to communicate about their actions, decisions, problems in the use of the tools, and decisions, as well as the finished product.

3. *Seeding:* providing materials that stimulate and support children in their self-directed activities in centers and projects.

The dual challenge of strengthening the content and skills in language and literacy development and those in creative expression/aesthetic development requires maintaining a balance between adult-guided and child-directed activities.

A DEVELOPMENTAL PERSPECTIVE

Children draw upon a diverse range of mental images when they are in the process of constructing meaning symbolically, either through expressive art or narrative language (Arnheim, 1969; Lowenfeld, 1957). As the processes of learning evolve, children use prior knowledge, skills, and experiences to develop various repertoires for artistic and linguistic growth. In the worlds of art and literacy education, there is a general consensus that growth in children's expressive art and communicative abilities occurs in tandem with the richness of their experiences and the stimulation from others to share their impressions and feelings (National Board for Professional Teaching Standards, 2000). To us, this means that in order to strengthen the use of language and media materials as modes of communication, we are challenged to enrich the children's well of experiences from which the content of communication flows.

Oral Language Development

Communication through a spoken language system develops from infancy progressively over time, beginning with expressions surrounding physical

> Children draw upon a diverse range of mental images when they are in the process of constructing meaning symbolically, either through expressive art or narrative language.

and emotional needs and then, with growth in language competence, increasingly embracing more complex kinds of messages. They discover how to communicate by experimenting with language, listening to the language of adults, and making approximations on the way to acquiring the standard language of the culture within which they are growing up (Ruddell & Ruddell, 1995). Preprimary children enter school having had several years' experience acquiring and using the spoken language that is common to their home culture.

Written Language Development

Similarly, children's ability to use the written language system develops over time (Clay, 1991; Harste, Woodward, & Burke, 1982). They progress from scribbling on any surface to controlling their scribbles with some degree of accuracy. Many children come to school familiar with some of the writing tools and the knowledge that writing conveys meaning. With experience they increase their knowledge and understanding of the writing tools and written symbols by experimenting, watching adults model the act of writing, and interacting with adults as they write. As with oral language, children's writing attempts begin with gross approximations of standard writing. Multiple experiences with text and opportunities to write for authentic purposes support the achievement of the ability to produce standard letter formations (Ferreiro & Teberosky, 1982).

Development in Using Expressive Art Materials

Just as children's increased fluency with oral and written language enhances their ability to communicate, so too does the ability to use the media materials to expand communication options. Children's initial introduction in school to the use of most expressive art materials, including plastic, graphic, printing, collage, and construction materials, occurs when an adult or peer models and/or explains how to use them in a variety of ways. The experimentation that follows primarily focuses on discovering "what happens when," experimenting with possibilities, and becoming aware of one's own personal reactions to the outcomes (Brearley, 1970). A typical example of this experimentation with media materials is shown in Photo 8.1. The child is beginning to experiment with the relationship between the placement of the paint on the paper, moving the brush on the paper resulting in the appearance of various shapes, and what happens when you mix colors. As with oral and written language, the ability to use media materials for expression becomes more controlled and sophisticated with expertise and support.

PHOTO 8.1

STANDARDS IN LANGUAGE AND LITERACY
AND THE EXPRESSIVE ARTS

The published standards in literacy, although stated in a variety of ways, essentially carry the same messages. In the areas of oral communication, the performance standards specify speaking and listening goals in the following general terms:

- In speaking, shares ideas, opinions, personal experiences, wishes, feelings, and requests information.
- Listens with understanding to conversations, directions, rhymes, and stories. Understands and follows simple multi-step directions.

Performance standards in reading and writing are also very general:

- Makes connections between oral and written language, reads and draws signs, and reads and writes some text.
- Understands the need to use different forms of recording for different purposes, such as drawing, charts, and conventional writing.

The standards in the area of the expressive arts deal not only with the use of art media materials but also with music—movement, song, listening to, and using instruments—and drama. In this chapter we focus only on the use of media materials as a form of communication. In the use of the visual art materials, the standards deal with the two levels of competence described earlier:

> **It is interesting to note that the standards in both literacy and the expressive arts converge on the development of the ability to communicate.**

- Increase the ability to use different media materials in a variety of ways.
- Expand abilities in drawing, painting, making models, and other art products that reflect personal perceptions, impressions, and experiences.
- Grow in understanding of artistic products of others.

It is interesting to note that the standards in both literacy and the expressive arts converge on the development of the ability to communicate (Cornett, 1998). Take, for example, the following expressive arts standards statements:

- Use oral language to describe or explain art.
- Understand and share opinions about others' artistic products and experiences.
- Appreciate listening to a variety of explanations about others' artistic products and experiences (Pennsylvania Department of Education and Department of Public Welfare, *Pennsylvania Learning Standards for Early Childhood*, 2009).

Similarly, the standards statements in language and literacy emphasize communication through all modalities:

- Communicate experiences, ideas, needs, choices, and feelings by speaking.
- Listen with understanding to conversations.
- Describe and share their own experiences.
- Demonstrate the behaviors of a beginning writer.
- Look for meanings in visual symbols (New York City Department of Education, *Prekindergarten Performance Standards*, 2003).

Since communication requires using a common language to receive, transmit, and exchange messages, our ability to strengthen content in the literacy and expressive arts centers rests in increasingly expanding mutual understandings of oral and written language meanings and the content of messages embedded in expressive art products.

SETTING UP AND SEEDING
THE LITERACY AND EXPRESSIVE ARTS CENTERS

The broad selection of materials in the literacy and expressive art centers provide opportunities for children to expand their abilities to produce their own messages and enjoy the messages of others. Typically, the area in and around the literacy center incorporates a library, listening center, and writing resource center. Materials in the library include books of different genres and topics and props for reenacting stories. The listening center includes a tape recorder or a CD player and both commercial and teacher-made tapes and CDs. The writing resource center includes materials for writing, drawing, and stamping. The expressive arts center resources offer the choices of molding materials (clay and play doh), graphic materials (paints, crayons, and markers), and collage and paper construction materials. The materials in each of these centers is usually rotated based on the current curriculum interests, themes, and activities associated with holidays and seasons. For example, around Valentine's Day, a center may be seeded with envelopes and blank cards and a set of children's name cards for reference as a follow-up to children's expressed interests in making Valentine cards.

EXPERIMENTING AND DISCOVERING WITH MEDIA MATERIALS

At the experimenting and discovering stage in which learning about the materials dominates the activity, there is no need for a common language relative to a creative or expressive message. There is, however, a need to help children clarify what they are discovering. Take children who work with clay in order to identify its properties. In Photo 8.2 we see a child focusing on collecting information about how clay behaves when manipulated and inventing ways she can change the shape of the clay. At the moment she is not expressing an interest in sharing the results of shaping and reshaping the clay with the adult.

In Photo 8.3 the youngster who has already experimented with molding clay in its usual state is immersed in discovering how clay behaves when it is very wet. His discovery that the clay sticks to his hands when it is very wet is so fascinating that he continues to manipulate the clay on his hands and subsequently seeks to share it with an adult nearby. "Look. Look." The language provided by an adult that can help a child be able to describe the properties of objects serves the communication purposes at this point:

"I see. The wet clay is sticking to your hands. Before you added the water it didn't stick like that, did it?"

PHOTO 8.2

The ability to increase understanding of the possibilities for using clay as a medium for expression depends upon an understanding of the factors that affect the moldability of clay.

It is quite likely that, at these beginning stages of experimenting and discovering, the children are intuitively changing their actions to find out more, but they are not yet able to articulate their growing understandings. The bridge between discovery and communication built by adult comments increases the likelihood that the children will be able to share what they have discovered with peers and others, and gain greater control over the use of the medium. In another example, Photo 8.4, the child is engaged in figuring out how to connect the straws and pipe cleaners and as a result is, by chance, creating geometric shapes. A comment such as, "I noticed that when you put

PHOTO 8.3   **PHOTO 8.4**

> **At the discovery stage in the use of the media materials,**
> **the first outcome is serendipitous—that is, it just happens.**

three straws together you made a triangle, and then you made a square with four straws," contributes to a child's ability to figure out how to purposefully create and construct shapes.

At the discovery stage in the use of the media materials, the first outcome is serendipitous—that is, it just happens. When children keep repeating how they use the materials to achieve the same outcome, it is no longer an accident of chance but rather a purposeful testing of the information they are collecting. This accounts for the fact that we often see young children repeating the same actions and getting the same results with the media materials a number of times before they change the actions—for example, snipping with a scissors again and again on the edge of a paper, or repeatedly causing the paint to drip down the paper on the easel with a saturated paintbrush.

Most of the information children collect during this discovery period with media materials falls into the category of science and mathematics learnings. They are identifying the unique properties of the materials and the results of using special tools with the materials, such as a rolling pin with the play-dough. Some of the properties they may discover are: crayon color appears darker the harder one presses on the crayon; long rolls of clay maintain their shape in a horizontal position, but not in the vertical position; the length of one scissors cutting action is limited, often requiring several cuts to complete severing the paper.

During the period when children are discovering and experimenting with possibilities, the potential for strengthening content learning lies in using oral language to clarify the effects of actions on outcomes. For example,

> *"I noticed that you turned the brush when you were painting and you made a wider line and then you turned it again and made a thinner line."*

In this instance, the adult is putting into words the child's actions, allowing for further conversation about purposefully controlling the medium in a timely way.

> *"If you wanted to make another wider line, how would you hold the brush?"*

With extended experience, as the child shows understanding of how to make different thickness in the lines, the adult can help the child make a generalization—that is, the position of the brush when painting makes a difference in the thickness of the lines.

FROM DISCOVERY TO
EXPRESSING WITH MEDIA MATERIALS

Once children's knowledge accumulates about the materials and how they behave, their products change from discovering how to control the media materials to pursuing interests in expressing their individual messages. The variety of messages chosen by children to communicate flow from their life experiences, specifically, how they interpret those experiences. The family is a typical subject that stimulates drawing and painting. Recently we watched as a child named each family member as she drew the picture. When she was finished she said to the teacher who was nearby: "This is my mommy but she has yellow hair because there isn't any brown paint." As she pointed to the green surrounding the figures, she said, "The walls are really blue but there is no blue paint." The teacher chatted with the child about these differences.

This child was explaining the meaning of her picture, clarifying details that the paints did not let her reproduce. When she got home she reported to her mother that she had painted her family, explaining once again the reasons for the difference between the colors she used and the real-life colors. Active listening by the adults advances the desire to talk about one's media representations.

When given opportunities to use media materials for drawing, painting, molding, and pasting we can expect children to represent a wide variety of subjects. The expressive art products in Photo 8.5 illustrate the wide variety of interests that show up in children's self-directed work. Here we see typical subjects of interest to this age group, self and other persons, animals and plants, environmental objects, and designs made from the

PHOTO 8.5

arrangement of collage materials. We also see the range in ability to represent these subjects.

At the stage in which children's discovery of ways to use the materials progresses to more purposeful representations of images and impressions, our role changes. Now it becomes important to shift from giving feedback on observed actions to stimulating more interaction about the meanings in the messages. When children begin to use the media materials to represent images in their heads, the oral language links to the messages they are communicating take on a new function. We are no longer confined to talking about discoveries of ways to use the materials, but are now concerned with helping the child use spoken language to talk about the message.

As described in earlier chapters, children value the opportunity to talk with the adult. They want to share. "Look at my monster." "I made a forest." "See what I did. I made a snake." Although they also enjoy adult praise, such as "I really like your snake," this kind of response does not encourage further conversation. Nor does it afford us the opportunity to bring content into view. Instead, a comment such as, "That is a really long snake, longer than the one you made before," opens up a series of possibilities. It might invite an action response, making the snake even longer, or lead to a conversation about the child's experiences with snakes. That, in turn, could spark a search for pictures of snakes and books about snake habitats. In this instance, the child may have realized the similarity of the rolled-out clay to a snake, or intentionally made a snake. What is important is to capitalize on the child's interest in sharing a discovery or product in order to expand the content potential offered by the child through the representation of an idea (Eisner, 1990; Scheinfeld, Haigh, & Scheinfeld, 2008).

PROMOTING COMMUNICATION IN CURRICULUM ACTIVITIES

As children move into purposeful representations of their world they increasingly begin to respond to the stimulation provided by adults to communicate through language and the use of media materials. Providing that stimulation through planned curriculum activities extends possibilities for transforming images and impressions about new content into language and media products.

The professional literature is replete with suggestions for single and sequenced sets of curriculum activities that will contribute to children's emerging abilities to communicate through language and the expressive arts (Garrison, 1979). Teachers continuously use these professional resources to add to their repertoire. Often, these activities evolve from the study of topics or themes through an integrated curriculum. Designs for integrated curriculum flow from theoretic perspectives, such as those of Reggio Emilia (Scheinfeld, Haigh, & Scheinfeld, 2008; Wien, 2008) and the Project Approach (Helm & Beneke, 2003). The activities offer rich opportunities to promote oral, written, and media expression. Typically, these include trips, literature, classroom visitors, celebrations, science projects, and special events in the lives of individual children in the class (Harlen, 1992; Kamii, 2000; Schickendanz, 2008; Williams, 1995; Williams, Rockwell, & Sherwood, 1987). Although curriculum activities stimulate the use of literacy and media materials, teachers find it challenging to maintain a balance between strengthening content and supporting children's creativity. If we enter at the wrong moment children may stop creating. If we do not enter their thinking we may miss an opportunity to strengthen a content understanding. This is the same challenge of timeliness of entry that has arisen in considering the potential for capitalizing on content possibilities in each of the other interest centers discussed in this book. Our answer lies in assuring that there are continuing opportunities for children to process the experiences in their own way.

STIMULATING CREATIVE EXPRESSION

What we have come to understand is that in addition to exposing children to new content and skills through activities that capture their interest, there are a series of developmental experiences that we can offer to increase their representational abilities and ultimately nurture creative expression. These developmental experiences focus children's attention on details of what they are observing or the unique attributes of the materials they are using. For example, the study of professional artists' blending of watercolors to create effects sensitizes children to the possibilities of manipulating colors or the study of body parts and their shapes leads to the children's awareness of using those shapes when drawing figures.

The products of their initial efforts at applying the new ideas will tend to be similar. Until the children become more adept at the use of the technique, their work will not have the same rich variety associated with our notions of creativity. It is not a question of whether to provide developmental experiences but rather how to interest children in participating and how to space the experiences so that children have the opportunity to incorporate the techniques into their own work. Mandated exposure to experiences that reveal how artists achieve effects without respect for children's interests is usually counterproductive.

> Mandated exposure to experiences that reveal how artists achieve effects without respect for children's interests is usually counterproductive.

Similarly, overloading children with new information fails to produce the desired long-term learning outcomes. The indicators of effectiveness in stimulating expressive abilities are children's incorporation of new learnings in their center activities in ways that expand their ability to communicate.

There is a fine line between using developmental experiences to foster meaning-making by each individual child and that of structuring the "processing" route for all of the children. The general guide to avoid the dangers of limiting children's opportunities for interpreting experiences in their own way is either to (1) present the materials and invite the children to create their own product, or (2) present the product and invite children to choose the materials they will use. A prescription of materials might be the use of clay to make an object of one's own choosing related to a class experience. A prescription of a product might be to make a decoration for a class party using any of the media materials on the shelves. This approach is most likely to avoid patterned or copycat products. However, if the children's products look very much the same, it is likely due to their inexperience with most of the materials or their lack of stimulation in thinking of possibilities for how to use them.

There is extensive literature that describes age appropriate approaches to art education and the visual arts for young children (Althouse, Johnson, & Mitchell, 2003; Douglas & Jaquith, 2009; Lowenfeld, 1957; Mulcahey, 2009; Pelo, 2007; Schirrmacher, 1993; Thompson, 2005). Viewing art as an integral part of early childhood education, these books provide teachers with ways to (1) help children appreciate the work of artists, (2) increase their skills of observation, and (3) refine their ability to express ideas, impressions, and emotions using media materials. The valued content in all of these resources is how creative expression experiences contribute to the ability to communicate and develop an appreciation for the arts.

SAMPLE DEVELOPMENTAL EXPERIENCES

Teachers often use books to stimulate children's thinking about ideas that capture their interest, thereby linking literacy and the expressive arts. One popular area for the selection of books is shape geometry, partly because the topic translates easily into engaging activities with media materials. The following vignettes illustrate a sequence of increasingly more complex activities that fit into the category of "developmental" because of their clear focus on educating the children's ability to discriminate the attributes of shape. The activities strengthen content about shape geometry as the children apply their understandings in unique ways using media resources. In the first vignette, the teacher involved children in a pasting activity, using triangles, following several experiences working with collections of shapes. The second vignette describes a set of activities children pursued after looking at and talking about ideas in the book *When a Line Bends—A Shape Begins* (Greene, 2001). The teacher followed this experience with another set of activities after reading the book *The Shape of Things* (Dodds, 1996). The geometric shape resources offered in the expressive art center were specifically selected in order for children to create their own pictures as a follow-up to looking at the books and sharing their ideas. The culminating activity for each set of events involved children in strengthening literacy development by talking about their products and the teacher modeling writing as she took their dictation. A bulletin board display of the products preceded putting them together in book form to add to the class library.

The descriptions of the activities that were primarily pursued in the literacy and expressive arts centers illustrate the interactive relationship between experience, representation, and language, along with a clear focus on content. Although the introduction of these activities is quite common in prekindergarten and kindergarten classrooms, the emphasis on developing conversations involving content in the context of the ongoing activities is not as common.

Vignette #1: Making Pictures with Triangles

This activity took place in the late fall. The teacher explained that the children had been learning about geometric shapes by matching and grouping identical shapes. She decided to place some cutout triangles in varied colors and sizes in the expressive art center and invite children who were interested to construct different shapes by using the triangles. Several children responded. After they pasted the cutout triangles on a piece of construction paper, they talked about their pictures while the teacher recorded their comments. Then she asked them if they would like to draw a copy of what they made on a separate piece of paper. Again they talked about the collage picture and the drawn picture comparing them.

Photos 8.6 and 8.7 illustrate the way that children uniquely use similar materials to express personal impressions of experience. Their labels of the objects they represent come from images in their head for which we are rarely able to track down the initial source. One child labeled the illustrations in her picture (Photo 8.6) as: "a ribbon like a bow." In Photo 8.7, the child

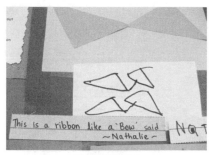

PHOTO 8.6

PHOTO 8.7

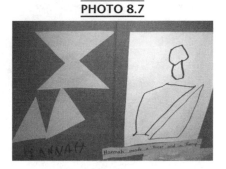

labeled the illustrations "a timer, and a ramp." Other images children labeled in their representations were a crocodile mouth (which the child called a "crocodile snap") and a boat. Children's ability to replicate their pasted pictures by drawing them reflects their understanding of the triangle as a basic form in their pictures.

As so often happens in early childhood classrooms, the work of a few children sparked an interest in others to try their hand at the same kind of activity. After displaying their work on the bulletin board, a book was created for the class library. Children were able to use the book for recalling their experience and sharing it with others. In this instance, the use of a class-made book in the library center helped move the children toward the literacy standards about book and print concepts, like

- identifies front/back cover,
- understands L-R directionality movement of text,
- uses illustrations as clues to text,
- identifies words/letters,
- understands that the print carries a message,
- shows real interest in books.

Vignette #2: Experimenting with Lines

The teacher read the book *When a Line Bends—A Shape Begins* (Greene, 2001). She talked with the children about comparing and contrasting the shapes of lines and asked them to think about/talk about what they saw when looking at differently shaped lines. Their responses to the curved line displayed in Photo 8.8 shows the different personal connections they made with a curved line. After talking about each shaped line and what it reminds them of, the teacher recorded their comments on separate pages, then the pages were put together to make a book for the class library.

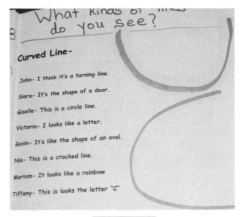

What kinds of lines do you see?

Curved Line—

John- I think it's a turning line.

Siara- It's the shape of a door.

Giselle- This is a circle line.

Victoria- I looks like a letter.

Gavin- It's like the shape of an oval.

Nia- This is a crooked line.

Mariam- It looks like a rainbow

Tiffany- This is looks the letter "C"

PHOTO 8.8

PHOTO 8.9

As an extension activity, the pages of the book were read into a tape recorder by the teacher. The children listened to the tape and looked at the book in the listening center. Later, the teacher talked to the children at the center about adding any other impressions they had about the various shaped lines.

She then invited the children who were interested to go to the expressive art center and draw their lines of choice. As they completed their lines, she invited them to use media materials to cover their line. See Photo 8.9 for a sample of a child's use of a rigid material to cover a zigzag line.

As a way of helping children value their involvement in center activity, she took their photographs while they were working with the materials. After she shared their products at group time, she placed them on the bulletin board along with the photos. Ultimately the children helped make a class book of their work entitled "When a line bends a shape begins."

As the children reviewed this activity with the teacher, she thought about other activities that might be developed in other centers, such as audio-taping the text of the book as a resource for listening in the library center. The study of the shape of lines led to observing the kinds of lines that make up letters: straight lines, curved lines, and circles. Identifying the kinds of lines that made up individual letters fed the emerging writing skills of the children as they pursued classroom activities in writing their own names, using functional writing approximations to make lists, labels, signs, and names of individuals in center activities.

Vignette #3: Using Precut Shapes

After reading the book *The Shape of Things* (Dodds, 1996), the teacher launched a conversation about favorite places and the shape of things in their favorite places. This curriculum activity followed the same pattern as the previous one. Children were invited to pursue thinking about the shape of things in the expressive art center where precut shapes, crayons, and collage materials had been provided. After creating their pictures, they shared their products with one another and the teacher. Then the teacher displayed them on the bulletin board along with pictures she had taken of the children at work making their pictures. Although the content of some of the children's representations were similar to that in the book, in all cases they added their own interpretation. In Photo 8.10, the use of the triangles to represent the mountains and the tree were different from any pictures in the book.

The content embedded in these three activities that the teacher used in conversations throughout the sequence included:

Geometry:

- attributes of shapes and their position/orientation and relative location
- part-whole relationship of lines and circles in shapes
- identification of similarities and differences in familiar shapes

Number and Measurement:

- comparative size, length, quantity

PHOTO 8.10

Brandon made mountains with snow on top. He also made a tree.

Literacy:

- vocabulary, names of geometric shapes and alphabet letters
- narrative descriptions of products
- narrative tales about experiences related to the books and completed work
- concepts about print

Science:

- discrimination between rigid and flexible materials to cover different line formations
- selection of materials with different properties to achieve effects

The last two vignettes illustrated the way in which book experiences can inspire oral language, written language, and media expression in both the literacy and expressive arts center. As mentioned above, other experiences that promote communication skills include trips, visitors, celebrations, theme-related activities, science projects, and special events in the lives of individual children in the class. The following are vignettes of science events that led to an increase in the use of communication skills.

EXPRESSING IDEAS IN RESPONSE TO SCIENCE EVENTS

Experimental work on imagery shows that images are not replications but reconstructions, which may involve additions, omissions and distortions. . . . images are essentially symbols of experiences.
—Sir Fredric Bartlett, "Art: Representation and Expression," p. 40

Experiences with science events also serve as developmental experiences in stimulating expressive art and language development. Observations translate into mental images which are processed in terms of meaning to the individual. When transforming the mental image to representation, individual interpretations drive the choice of the details to represent. When children talk about and record observations as illustrated in the following examples, they are transforming perception to mental images and then to representation, which can again be described through language. If they are capturing a moment in time, the opportunity to compare the representation with other children's representations and with the original object, encourages further looking and thinking about what they have observed. In one classroom where the children were studying the life cycle of butterflies, the teacher placed the jar with a chrysalis in the science center. As children stopped to view the display, they were invited to draw a picture of what they saw. After several children had completed their drawings, the teacher encouraged them to compare the representations for similarities and differences, and then to look again at the chrysalis in the jar. In addition to the obvious science content, this activity strengthened the content in both literacy and the expressive arts by the children's use of language for comparing and contrasting representations of the chrysalis and the focus on discovering differences in their representations of the same object due in part to what the *artist* saw.

If children make a series of representations of change over time, as illustrated in the following vignette, they can use these representations to compare and contrast their record of events with others who recorded the same events.

Vignette #4: Planting Grass Seeds

The children were noticing that the grass was beginning to grow on the playground. The grass seed planting activity in the classroom involved the children placing grass seeds on sponges and adding water. The teacher then began a routine of examining the seeds every few days and engaging individual children in describing and illustrating what was happening. The children's drawings revealed how they were interpreting their observations in communication modes, namely, expressive arts and language. The teacher added the written language as another form of permanent record for the children. In the early stages of sprouting, the children talked about the lack of change that they were able to discern. "I only see the seeds, no grass." Some gave reasons for the lack of change, for example, "It looks the same way because we have to put more water."

After the seeds sprouted, the children's drawings and observations reflected the same diversity in both oral and graphic representation.

Picture of a sponge and some grass: *"My sponge is growing into grass."*

Picture of long blades of grass on a sponge: *"My grass is getting bigger and bigger and it [is] going to reach up to the sky."*

Picture of 10 blades of grass growing out of the sponge: *"It's growing ten seed grass."*

Picture of lots of grass sprouts: *"It's a miracle my grass is growing."*

The content embedded in this activity is similar to the earlier one. Here the children are having repeated experiences in observing, describing, and recording changes over a period of time using oral language and media representations and sharing their interpretation of these changes both in the way they represent them and describe them.

As shown in these two vignettes, science activities are another vehicle for giving children developmental experiences that lead to increasing children's skills of observation and refining their ability to communicate ideas and impressions using language and media materials.

SUMMARY

The activities in the literacy and expressive art centers serve a unique function in the development of communication abilities of young children. These two centers offer them the opportunity to represent stories, experiences, and ideas through the use of a variety of media materials, as well as oral and written text.

The developmental sequence begins with exposure to opportunities to experiment with oral and written language as well as to find out about how to use media materials. It continues with the provision of focused experiences to expand children's horizons. Developmental experiences are provided to increase their observational skills and strengthen their ability to communicate through language and the expressive art medium. With continued opportunities to use the skills they are developing for functional purposes, children will use oral and written text as well as media representations with more precision. In an environment in which children often use the expressive arts and literacy materials, we will see writing emerging as children make connections between a rich set of experiences and their need to express how they are processing and responding to these experiences. In this way we nurture their ability to meet the standards in literacy and the expressive arts, as illustrated in Photo 8.11.

PHOTO 8.11

CHAPTER 9

Assessing Children's Learning: Documenting Results for Accountability Purposes

As discussed in the first chapter of this book, major stakeholders who oversee the early childhood community want proof that children are acquiring the learnings spelled out in standards documents that have been adopted by their school, community, city, or state, regardless of the curricula or teaching methods used. This means that, in addition to achieving our goal of intentionally increasing the focus on content and embedding academic skills in a meaningful context for children, we are obliged to provide evidence that the children do acquire those key content ideas and academic skills required to succeed at the next grade level (Bredekamp, 1987; Shepard, Kagan, & Wurtz, 1998). The purpose of this chapter is to share with the reader our approach to collecting and recording evidence of children's learning in a content rich, action-based program using the language of the standards. We have selected literacy and mathematics for our focus in this chapter because it is the dominant criteria for evaluating success in school programs even though we firmly believe that evaluative criteria for early childhood programs should be much broader.

There is little question that assessment for accountability purposes in prekindergarten and kindergarten classrooms is a "hot-button" issue. The controversy does not lie in the notion of "assessing." For decades, early childhood teachers have been assessing children's progress for the purpose of supporting their development and learning, as discussed in Chapter 3. The controversy lies in how to appropriately assess young children for "accountability" purposes. The issue takes shape with the selection of assessment instruments that are deemed suitable for this age group (Wortham, 2001). On one side of the issue, there are those who seek to eliminate all but observational assessments until children are 7–8 years old, judging other

> There is little question that assessment for accountability purposes in prekindergarten and kindergarten classrooms is a "hot-button" issue.

forms as developmentally inappropriate (Almy & Genishi, 1979; Boehm & Weinberg, 1996; Bredekamp & Rosegrant, 1992; Cohen, Stern, & Balaban, 2008; McAfee, Leong, & Bodrova, 2004). On the other side are those who firmly believe that we have an obligation to use standardized instruments to assess young children's progress in mastering the school skills because they give us valid and reliable information as to what each child has learned.

We take the position that the assessment process needs to include a series of procedures that simultaneously conforms with our understanding of children's growth, development and learning and also equips us to report the results to major stakeholders to meet their expectations. The process begins with observation of children in self-directed activities and proceeds to increasingly engaging them in activities shaped by others from which we can obtain additional assessment information. Through this progression, assessment information can be captured in an organized and easily retrievable format for reporting purposes.

THE ASSESSMENT PROGRESSION

Observing children as they pursue their own interests is not a new phenomenon in early childhood classrooms. For more than half a century, the field of early childhood education has promoted teacher observation as a way to obtain information and build understandings to help them more effectively support each individual child's development and learning (Beaty, 1986; Genishi, 1992; Good & Brophy, 2008; Hartley, Frank, & Goldenson, 1952; Jablon, Dombro, & Dichtelmiller, 2007; Meisels et al., 2001; Wortham, 2001). The importance of the information gained from observation lies in the fact that much of it is acquired while children are in natural settings, showing us what they know and can do as they pursue their own interests in events they have crafted.

It is well documented in the literature that observing young children in action gives us data not only about their social-emotional development but also about the skills and content understandings they are using to serve their own purposes during self-directed activities (Ginsberg, Inoue, & Seo, 2008; Reynolds & Jones, 1997; Wann, Dorn, & Liddle, 1962). The current challenge, as we see it, is to document observations of children's skill development and content understanding in more planful ways so that the data provides the kind of information that can be used to convince policymakers that action-based settings are rich with content and also nurture the acquisition of conventional skills.

It is generally accepted that the use of a well-organized system for recording information obtained through observation notes, examinations of children's work samples, and media recordings can serve as the basis for reporting children's progress. However, in our view, an assessment system that relies solely on observational data gleaned from children working in natural

> The current challenge, as we see it, is to document observations of children's skill development and content understanding in more planful ways so that the data provides the kind of information that can be used to convince policymakers that action-based settings are rich with content and also nurture the acquisition of conventional skills.

settings does not provide sufficient information about a child's knowledge and skill development.

Children who show us they have a skill in a certain area while working independently with materials–for example, counting out loud to eight while making a tower with table blocks–may not be able to demonstrate they have the same skill when an adult makes a request, such as collecting eight straws for distribution during snack. The child's thinking for these two tasks flows from different sources. The first task calls for using numbers to organize one's own self-directed actions, while the second task requires the use of numbers to follow a task of someone else's choosing (Donaldson, 1978). Therefore, before we are comfortable in declaring that a child has mastered a particular skill that meets a standard, we are responsible for ensuring mastery of the skill in both contexts; during self-guided activity and in response to an external request or an activity designed by others.

SOURCES OF ASSESSMENT DATA

As already discussed, the initial source of assessment data flows from observations of children as they pursue their own interests in centers. This is followed by collecting information from children's responses to tasks within (1) teacher-directed management activities and (2) teacher-designed curriculum activities. This kind of data provides information on children's ability to use what they know and can do in response to an external request. Teachers have long used management tasks as sources of assessment information. They target such skills as name recognition and shape discrimination. For example, they ask a child to find her name card and return it to the name chart, or they ask a child to sort table blocks by shape during clean-up. They have also designed curriculum activities that include embedded tasks to reveal assessment information on a standard. For example, asking a child to make up a simple rhyme to add to the class collection of rhymes provides assessment information on the child's phonemic awareness.

> An assessment system that relies solely on observational data gleaned from children working in natural settings does not provide sufficient information about a child's knowledge and skill development.

Whether the teacher-designed tasks occur during management events or are a part of a curriculum activity, they reveal information on children's use of skills in explicit and focused ways. Children's performance on targeted tasks either confirms observations about a child's skill acquisition or alerts us that the skill is not yet stable. This means that it will take more time to develop consistency in use. Once young children evidence mastery of tasks that have been embedded in teacher-designed curriculum activities or management tasks, it is reasonable to initiate experiences that represent standard tasks, such as asking children individually to collect all the letters from a set that they can name. This kind of assessment task provides reliable information that meets accountability demands about letter recognition for every child who was requested to perform the task.

Only when children demonstrate fluency in using skills for a variety of purposes in contexts they understand can we consider posing tasks that ask them to produce the skills for reasons they cannot understand. For example, while a child is waiting to be picked up at the end of the day, ask a question "out of the blue," like "If you have five marbles and I give you three more, how many would you have?" Familiarizing children with out-of-context tasks prepares them for the future when they will be required to take "tests," in the form of norm-referenced and validated standardized assessment instruments. If we have successfully followed the first two stages in the progression of collecting assessment data, and verified that children are stable in their use of targeted academic skills, the results of the "on-demand" teacher assessments in isolated contexts will confirm that children have met the standards in a manner that the world outside of the classroom deems valuable.

COLLECTING OBSERVATIONAL DATA:
PHASE 1 IN THE PROGRESSION

The job of recording observations usually poses serious challenges to teachers in terms of time invested and payoff. Historically, the field has placed a great deal of emphasis on the use of anecdotal recordings to construct profiles of children that encompasses large segments of development and/or learning, such as language, or social-emotional development. For the purposes of this initiative, we are looking to organize these recordings

Only when children demonstrate fluency in using skills for a variety of purposes in contexts they understand can we consider posing tasks that ask them to produce the skills for reasons they cannot understand.

by creating effective, accurate, and useable data collection procedures that target the standards.

In order to accomplish this goal, there are three steps in the process. Step One deals with collecting the evidence by observing and recording information while children are engaged with materials. Step Two involves organizing the information collected during observation in a systematic way so that it is easily retrievable for different purposes. At Step Three we culminate the task by evaluating the information we have collected against such criteria as content standards, or lists of skills that are valued by the school or community for accountability purposes.

STEP ONE: Collecting the Evidence

In addition to the familiar procedure of jotting down notes of observations on children's spontaneous use of the academic skills that are usually included in performance standards, there are several other evidence sources. They include:

- work samples, for example, a piece of writing done spontaneously at an interest center such as a shopping list;
- photographs of a child's work, such as a picture of the barnyard that a child built in the block area where he paired each adult animal with its baby;
- video- or audiotapes, such as a child retelling a familiar story.

If the notations of observations and the other sources of evidence listed above are going to be useful for future analysis and accountability purposes, they need to include the knowledge observed. In addition, each observation also needs information of the context under which it was demonstrated.

STEP TWO: Organizing the Information

Effective use of the written notes, work samples, and photographs requires an efficient system for organizing the observational information, one that makes sense to the user and demands as little administrative time as possible. Teachers vary in their view of what constitutes "efficient." Some prefer commercial preprinted recording forms, one for each child or a class summary sheet. Others prefer to create their own recording forms, either one sheet per child listing all of the behavior indicators in a subject area or one sheet per standard with all children listed (e.g., "uses tallies and written numerals to represent numerical quantities"; see Appendix D). No matter which organizing format is selected, it needs to provide space for several entries collected over a period of time for each standard, skill, and/or a key idea in a content area in order to identify the level of achievement and the stability.

Commercial assessment systems that use observation as the primary source of data, provide guidelines for what information to collect and how to organize it. Typical examples of commercial assessment packages are *The Work Sampling System* (Meisels et al., 2009), and the *Child Observation Record* (High Scope Educational Foundation, 2003). Later on in this chapter, we will share with the reader several documentation forms developed with teachers and describe how they used them to record the development of children's acquisition of academic skills that are listed in many of the standards books.

STEP THREE: Analyzing the Information

Once observational data has been collected and organized in a systematic way, the next critical step is to examine the data in terms of the standards on which the children are being assessed. Without this step, the time and effort we so often use to collect and organize the information has no real application or practical purpose. In addition to meeting requirements related to accountability, the results of analysis serve the function of informing curriculum decisions that build upon children's strengths and address their needs.

Some standards lend themselves to easy analysis using observation data with little interpretation, such as "Reads and writes numerals to represent quantity." For these standards we can determine the child's ability to meet the standard with a check of "yes" or "no" accompanied by a notation of the number level achieved (e.g., up to 12). Other standards, however, are the culminating point of a developmental progression, and the child's behavior needs to be looked at in relation to the performance within the progression.

The use of a rubric that outlines the steps along the way to meeting the standard helps us pinpoint the child's development in achieving the standard over a period of time. Figure 9.1 provides an example of the use of a rubric for recording observations about linear measurement. The mathematics standard that this rubric is based on is "Understands that the physical properties of objects can be measured and compared using non-standard and/or standard units."

Rubrics that define the sequence of behaviors that reflect increasing mastery of the skill in each of the standards areas can be generated by classroom teachers or found in various curriculum texts. List of developmental sequences that serve as a basis for a rubric in the areas of Visual Discrimination, Auditory Discrimination, and Number Sense appear in Appendices J, K, and L.

FIGURE 9.1. Rubric for Linear Measurement

Sequence of Skills: Linear Measurement	Observational Recordings of Jorge's Action
Compares length of two objects.	*November:* compares two different-length straws and labels them "longer" and "shorter."
Uses a set of identical objects to measure length: non-standard measurement tools.	*December:* connects identical links and then measures the length of her shoe; counts and declares: "It's five links long."
Uses standard measurement tools: inch cubes.	*March:* uses inch cubes to measure identical length strips for use on a placemat; counts and declares "It's ten inches long."
Uses standard ruler.	*May:* uses a ruler to measure the length of feet of self and peers: "My foot is six inches long and his is seven."

DESIGNING ASSESSMENT TASKS IN MANAGEMENT AND CURRICULUM ACTIVITIES: PHASE 2 IN THE PROGRESSION

The next phase in the assessment process is to confirm that the findings we gleaned from observations in self-selected activities holds up in situations other than the one in which we observed it. In the daily life of the classroom, we ask children to do many tasks related to management events. Embedding the use of skills in these events will allow us to confirm the degree to which children have stabilized the learnings observed in the center-time activities. Over a period of days and weeks, all children can be given similar standards-related tasks in order to get uniform information.

In addition to purposefully assessing children's learning during the management activities of the program, curriculum activities need to be designed that will elicit actions in children that we can document for purposes of accountability. Just as in the management tasks, it is important to engage the children in activities with similar tasks in ways that allow them to individually demonstrate what they know and can do in relation to the targeted standard. For example, if the targeted standard is "understands patterns and relations," an activity that engages children in creating a border pattern for their own placemat for a party reveals each child's level of understanding of patterns.

The recording of assessment information gleaned from teacher-designed curriculum activities needs to coordinate with the information gained from observations during naturally occurring center activities related to a specific standard. Through this coordination, it is possible to identify the stability of the targeted skill. Once again, lack of stability drives planning for further curriculum experiences until mastery is achieved. Sample recording forms we generated for entering assessment information from both the naturally occurring events and the teacher-designed tasks in mathematics (number, geometry, measurement, and algebra), physical science, alphabetic knowledge, and visual discrimination, appear in Appendices M, N, O, and P.

The following examples of teacher-designed tasks illustrate the relationship between rubrics that list developmental stages in mastering a skill or key idea in a content area and the standards-related tasks.

Teacher-Designed Task for Assessing Development in the Ability to Retell a Story

In literacy, a group of prekindergarten teachers focused on collecting information on children's skills in retelling a story in sequence. They set the performance task as "retells" a four-event story in sequence based on the experiences of listening to the story twice during a 2-day period.

When teachers compared notes on their experiences of asking children to retell a story, it became clear that they had created different conditions for retelling and they did not share common criteria for rating success. The conditions varied from "retelling to the teacher without peers present," to "retelling in a small or large group setting." Some teachers provided props for retelling, others provided prompts, and still others created a collaborative climate in which the children chimed in as helpers for retelling the story. Based on these revelations, the teachers decided they wanted to add more detail to the recording form, which would standardize the assessment, and, in effect, create a rubric. Figure 9.2 is their final version of the story retelling rubric. As they analyzed children's skills, they recognized the steps in the progression from shared retelling to supported retelling and ending with independent retelling. This kind of experience of generating a rubric increased their understanding of the importance of clarifying not only the conditions under which the assessment task is performed, but also the developmental sequence.

Teacher-Designed Task for Assessing Development in Understanding Shape Geometry

Teachers considered possible items for a mathematics rubric dealing with shape geometry. The standard states "recognize properties and characteristics of geometric shapes" (Appendix D). They developed the following progression of behavior indicators toward meeting the standard:

- matches identical shapes
- groups similar shapes together (e.g. circles and ovals)
- classifies shapes (e.g., varied types of triangles)

FIGURE 9.2. Rubric for Retelling

Child's Name: _____   Date: _____

Title of Story: _____

Linguistic level: Uses Minimal Text Language ___

Uses Rich Text Language ___   **COMMENTS**

1. Opens retelling with a story context/event that sets the story in motion.

No Response   With Props   With Prompts   Independently

☐   ☐   ☐   ☐

2. Includes major/critical events in an order that builds the story line or plot.

No Response   With Props   With Prompts   Independently

☐   ☐   ☐   ☐

3. Clarifies major character roles.

No Response   With Props   With Prompts   Independently

☐   ☐   ☐   ☐

4. Includes minor events.

No Response   With Props   With Prompts   Independently

☐   ☐   ☐   ☐

5. Clarifies minor character roles.

No Response   With Props   With Prompts   Independently

☐   ☐   ☐   ☐

6. Brings story to closure appropriately as related to the events.

No Response   With Props   With Prompts   Independently

☐   ☐   ☐   ☐

This figure is available for free download and printing on the Teachers College Press website: www.tcpress.com

Information collected over a period of time using teacher-designed tasks might look like this:

October Task: Collect all the triangle pieces in a collection of mixed shapes during cleanup time (match identical shapes).

Martin: Collected the equilateral triangles, not the right triangles.

February Task: Sort a collection of mixed shapes for storage (group similar shapes).

Martin: Grouped large and small triangles together, and did the same with the squares and circles. Ignored the rectangles and hexagons.

May Task: Sort a mixed group of shapes of various sizes and colors into shape groups (classify shapes).

Martin: Placed all isosceles, right, and equilateral triangles in the same group irrespective of size and color. Did the same with circles. Placed squares and rectangles in the same group (recognizing the similarity in four-sided figures) irrespective of size and color. When asked, named the groups as *triangles, circles,* and *rectangles.*

Teacher-Designed Tasks for Assessing Development in the Ability to Write

Early childhood teachers generally agree that writing development is best assessed in the context of personal writing because ownership by the writer is important. A simple teacher-designed task, in terms of writing to determine correct letter formation, involves asking children to write their name on each piece of artwork they produce. For this standard, teachers were comfortable using a simple checklist with the following six headings: (1) random scribble, (2) controlled scribble, (3) letter-like symbols, (4) conventional letter formations, (5) letters of first name in sequence, (6) full name.

Asking children to draw and write about different kinds of class experiences provides samples to analyze how a child is moving into concepts about print and knowledge of sound-symbol relationships. What is important is that the task hold genuine interest for the child and that we create a risk-free setting for drawing and writing. For example, an invitation to children to choose their favorite part of the supermarket trip, draw a picture of it, and write about it for a class book usually generates considerable enthusiasm in the activity. A child's writing can be analyzed for correct letter formation in terms of the stages of writing listed above. It can also be analyzed to determine a child's progress in using sound-symbol relationships—moving from little or no knowledge of those relationships, through the stage of beginning to represent sound-symbol correspondence, and finally understanding that letters are associated with specific sounds that, when placed together, represent words. Writing can also be analyzed in terms of evidence of child's concepts about print (i.e., use of directionality, left-right and top-bottom, spacing between words, and punctuation).

Teacher-Designed Task for Assessing Development in Oral Language Expression and Writing

In the following vignette we share with the reader one of the ways in which a teacher pursued a popular activity coordinating expressive art with the collection of assessment information, specifically in the development of both oral language expression and letter formation and concepts about print. It illustrates how to obtain a range of assessment information from a high-interest activity that engages most of the children. Following reading *The Snowman Storybook* (Biggs, 1990), the teacher initiated a conversation with the children about their experiences with snow and invited them to make their own snowman pictures in the expressive art center during center time. As children completed their pictures, she asked them to talk about what they created, wrote down their dictated statements, and then invited them to rewrite the statement for themselves on the line below her writing.

Photos 9.1, 9.2, and 9.3 (shown on p. 134) illustrate the differences in development of 4- and 5-year-old children who have shared the same read-aloud and in-class discussions about an environmental event. The work of the three children provides a remarkable illustration of the links in terms of development between graphic representation of an idea, use of oral language, and writing skills.

In the first—Photo 9.1, the least sophisticated in terms of communication skills—the youngster is re-creating the most conventional representation of a snowman—three stacked circles—and makes a brief declarative statement about his product: "I make a snowman." He is using language to describe his picture. His description is accurate, although his grammar is non-standard. His writing, a wavy long line, illustrates that he has some sense that lines equate to written communication, but he has little understanding of the significance of discrete letters.

In the second, Photo 9.2, the child's picture has more detail in the face and body, her explanation goes beyond only describing what she did. Instead she shares her ideas about where snow comes from, giving us a window into her understanding of weather phenomena: "The snow comes from the sky." The language is limited but the grammar is correct. Her writing shows a beginning awareness of standard letter formation and the idea that strings of letters make words.

PHOTO 9.1

PHOTO 9.2

PHOTO 9.3

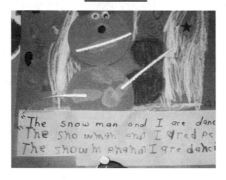

Finally, in the third, Photo 9.3, the child has turned to the dramatic possibilities, "The snowman and I are dancing." His picture of the snowman is more detailed, and he is using his language to define a relationship he has created in his mind. His writing shows a strong grasp of conventions of writing. He uses correct letter formation, spaces between words, and capitalizes the first word of a sentence. Although he is clearly using the written model to guide his writing, the difference in the way he writes and that of his peers in the first two photos demonstrates an awareness of concepts of print that his classmates have not yet achieved.

Teacher-Designed Task for Assessing Development in Understanding Spatial Geometry

The following is a sample of a teacher-designed task to meet the standard, "Understands location, position, and spatial relationships." The object of the task is to have children strategically place and paste precut shapes on a piece of paper in response to verbal directions about position. The teacher described the activity as follows:

> *I began the task by giving each child six different precut shapes and asking them to independently follow my specific directions about their placement on a piece of paper. After they had enjoyed the activity of placing their shapes in a specific location, I examined their work to assess their understanding of the directions. Then I invited each team of children to talk about what they had done, comparing results. "Do your pictures look the same? Are the shapes in the same positions?"*

Photo 9.4 shows the work of two of the children. Below is a record of what the children said about their pictures.

> *Nicholas:* My picture has the hexagon on the rectangle and Victoria's rectangle is next to the triangle. My triangle is crooked and her rectangle is not.
>
> *Victoria:* The pictures are different. His hexagon and rectangle look like a tree and mine doesn't look like the same.

The conversation provided additional assessment information about their ability to accurately name shapes and use positional and locational words.

PHOTO 9.4

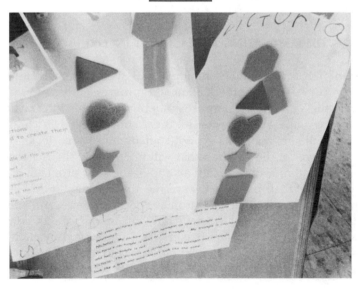

TEACHER-DESIGNED STANDARD TASKS:
PHASE 3 IN THE PROGRESSION

There is strong evidence that valid and reliable information collected through the use of formal assessments of young children's learning is difficult to obtain (Bredekamp, 1987; Shepard, Kagan, & Wurtz, 1998). Due to the unfamiliarity of the conditions that surround standardized tests, young children under the age of 7 often fail to reveal what they know and can do. Additionally, because they are inconsistent in communicating their understandings and demonstrating academic skills, any single round of test data is not necessarily reliable. Standardized tests often fall short of assessing those skills and learnings valued by districts or school leaders.

Through the observation of children's response to teacher-designed standard tasks, we are in a position to help them become increasingly aware of their own abilities and how they use them successfully in different kinds of situations. So, if in response to an out-of-context task such as "Please bring me twenty sheets of paper from the closet," the child brings the exact number requested, the teacher can now declare, "You really count to twenty very well. I hope you show your family how well you count to twenty." In essence, we are empowering children to "brag about what they know and can do." This, in turn, empowers them to use the skills they have developed in a variety of ways that is not necessarily dependent upon an immediately recognizable context. This is a way for us to help children develop a sense of confidence in their ability to show others what they know and can do when asked to perform tasks on standard assessments.

DISSEMINATING ASSESSMENT INFORMATION

Assessment for accountability requires that we adequately inform the different groups of stakeholders about the progress children are making in meeting the standards. There is a different need for information with the different groups. Parents want to know about their own child's progress throughout the year. The school staff usually wants to know about the learning level of the children that will be entering their classes in the next year. The administrators want an end-of-the-year profile of each class group in terms of their progress toward meeting the standards. Central office administrators want a school profile. Policy makers want community profiles. If we are to succeed in adequately informing parents, administrators, evaluators, public decision-makers, and the major stakeholders, we need to provide reliable documentation about how well the children are meeting the standards in easily understandable formats. The assessment information used for this purpose needs to be standardized in some way so that it represents accurate and reliable descriptions of children's performance behaviors in response to teacher-designed tasks and analyses of children's products produced under similar conditions. Checklists and the use of rubrics are the easiest for recording and summarizing this information. We need to keep in mind that checklists are the least informative for making curriculum and instruction decisions. However, they provide the most accessible information for accountability toward meeting academic skill development standards. The use of formats for dealing with accountability demands does not preclude the use of more comprehensive assessment tools to inform program decision-making.

SUMMARY

If we are to make our case that the action-based learning environment can empower children with the required skills and understandings specified in the various standards lists, it is essential that we nurture the development of these skills in meaningful contexts and document through informal as well as formal means their acquisition of the targeted standards. By capturing what children have learned and are able to do through observation and work samples that are collected in both naturally occurring and teacher designed tasks in a systematic way, we can provide evidence of developmental progress over time and document the power of this approach for others. The need to document what children are learning in action-based school settings also serves the purpose of bringing parents on board as supporters of the kind of learning environment that conforms with the developmental needs of the children and the academic expectations of the system.

CHAPTER 10

Next Steps for Strengthening Content and Teaching Practice in the Action-Based Learning Environment

In this book we have shared with the readers our work with preprimary teachers in order to contribute to the work already begun in the early childhood community to incorporate a rich array of content ideas into preprimary programs. Our goal in describing and documenting our work over the past 2 decades has been to increase that momentum already begun in the early childhood field to strengthen the preprimary curriculum and meet the standards within the context of an action-based learning environment.

Our primary goal has been to help early childhood teachers more clearly address their needs for defining the curriculum and documenting children's learning while maintaining the "child-centered" approach that values the importance of the daily scheduling of interest-center periods. Our concern and those of the teachers with whom we worked were that the pressure to replace the interest center periods with periods of direct instruction on conventional academic skills would drive changes in programs that do not serve the best interests of young children as learners.

The search for a design that could embed content and nurture academic skill development within an action-based program rested on the strong belief that the most enduring and sustaining learning for young children occurs through action and interaction with people and materials while pursuing interests in an emotionally and cognitively responsive environment.

Based on this view, our first task was to clarify the key content ideas that young children are generating and the academic skills they use in the variety of activities in which they engage. It is well documented that young children intuitively understand considerably more than they can explain. By observing and listening to them when they are pursuing their own interests, we have access to identifying some of those emerging understandings.

Although we cannot definitively identify the ideas they are constructing, we can nurture the process through conversation and provision of the language to help them formulate intuitive understandings. The three major routes available to us are (1) initiate a conversation during or directly after a child-directed activity in an interest center based on information obtained through observation, (2) enrich children's learning environments through the provision of materials in centers to feed content interests, and (3) provide enrichment activities that conform to an integrated curriculum model.

MEETING THE CHALLENGES

The first step toward the goal of strengthening curriculum has been to more precisely identify key ideas in the content areas that emerge as children pursue activities of high interest, whether self-directed or teacher-guided.

- The lists of key ideas in the content areas referred to throughout this book are works in progress. We expect that users of these lists will continue to refine and adapt them based upon increased understandings developed through use.

The second step involved clarification of the preprimary standards and behavioral indicators associated with these key ideas so we can recognize them through observation as they appear in children's activities.

- Since the list of performance standards and behavioral indicators vary in different locales and are interpreted in different ways, each school community faces the challenge of translating the curriculum expectations and standards into behavior sequences that emerge progressively when children have the opportunity to process experiences and use skills in self-directed activities.

The third step has proven to be one of the most challenging for teachers, that of initiating conversations with children about the content that was showing up in their actions without inadvertently distracting them from what they were doing. Increasing curriculum content and addressing the standards for children requires activating a teaching role that helps children clarify and expand ideas they are using in their activities. This strategy is distinguished from one in which teachers engage children in content-rich conversations during group instructional periods. We found that experienced early childhood teachers were skillful in guiding the children in their management of the social demands of group living and offering comments of appreciation for children's products that were completed in the centers. However, in our experience, they were not accustomed to initiating content conversations in the centers during center time.

- The challenge of helping children become more consciously aware of their own intuitive knowledge and building on that knowledge call for adaptation in teaching strategies. The many illustrations of conversational entries in each of the center chapters are intended to serve as examples. Through practice, readers will generate their own ways to pursue this route to initiating authentic conversation with a content emphasis.

The fourth step, that of building on children's expressed interests to expand the curriculum through topics and themes, was the most familiar and therefore the easiest. The additional feature of selecting key content ideas for planning theme activities and identifying behavioral indicators to guide observation proved to be stimulating and rewarding. The process of identifying content helped them sustain focus during the various theme-related activities. It also directed attention to planning for provision of resources in centers based on the notion that the constant interplay between exposure to new experiences and skills and meaning-making of the new experiences through one's own actions constitutes the core of children's learning.

- Developing the habit of linking key ideas in the content areas along with listing key vocabulary within the theme will require more planning time. Review and revision of plans after each implementation will sharpen this skill.

Finally, the fifth and last step involves documenting the children's progress toward the standards in ways that are valued by parents, the educational leadership, and policy makers in a specific school community. In our view, the tension between valuing observational information versus more objective checklists and other assessment tools can be reduced if they are viewed as occurring along a continuum that serves accountability demands. This continuum begins with recording children's use of content ideas and traditional academic skills as they pursue their own interests. It progresses to engaging children in using their understandings and skills in activities initiated by others in the larger curriculum context. Finally, after children demonstrate fluency in using those learnings deemed essential as they progress into the grades, we can consider documenting their learning through the more focused tasks.

- In order to protect against premature use of standardized tests, which have frequently proved to be unreliable and invalid, readers are challenged to devise procedures for documenting children's emerging understandings and skills that show progress over time toward meeting the standards. The sample forms in this book for documenting observations of children in action, followed by their performance in teacher-designed tasks, are intended to illustrate ways to meet accountability expectations for children in action-based programs. As members of the early childhood sector of school communities, it is critical that we document children's learning in ways that will influence policy decisions that conform with the way young children learn.

OUR CHALLENGE FOR THE FUTURE

We have come to understand that to successfully work at protecting the rights of young children to have the kind of school experiences that conform with their developmental learning patterns and needs, we are obliged to become more effective in implementing, documenting, and communicating not only "how children learn" but also "what they are learning" in action-based learning environments. We believe the momentum in efforts to strengthen curriculum and meet the standards for preprimary children that has developed over the past 2 decades holds great promise for achieving our goal of preserving the kind of environment that nurtures the lifelong learner. It is up to all of us to maintain this momentum.

Appendices

The listing of content ideas that young children can begin to develop and extend (Appendices A–F) are culled from the literature generated by national and state professional subject area organizations in mathematics, science, social studies, literacy and reading, and professional scholars in each of these areas. The performance standards and the behavior indicators connected to the content ideas are culled from a variety of state and local early childhood standards publications, and are adapted by the authors to make the content more usable.

Note: The content appendices and forms (Appendices A–F, H, and M–P) are available for free download and printing on the Teachers College Press website: www.tcpress.com

APPENDIX A

Physical Science Content

Key Content Ideas	Performance Standards and Behavior Indicators
PHYSICAL LAWS OF MOTION	
A force is needed to move an object. Forces include pushing and pulling; gravity; and moving air. Simple machines such as levers, gears, and pulleys reduce the amount of force needed to move objects.	*Recognizes that different forces move objects and asks questions about the forces.* *Understands that simple machines reduce the amount of force needed to move an object.* Purposefully experiments with ways to move objects with such actions as pushing, pulling, rolling, sliding, and dragging, and compares the results. Experiments with simple machines such as wheels and pulleys and talks about how it is easier to move an object.
The speed, distance, and direction of movement of an object are dependent upon the shape and surface of the object, the surface on which it moves, and the intensity of the force.	*Realizes that in addition to the force, differently shaped objects and the surface texture of both the object and the surface affect the speed, distance, and direction of movement of objects.* Purposefully adjusts the force to control speed, distance, and direction of movement and talks about how to control or change the movement. Selects a surface and an object to achieve a result—e.g., moves from the rug to the floor to speed the movement of miniature cars that are being pushed.
MATTER	
Objects have unique properties that distinguish them from one another and define the potential for use.	*Distinguishes objects by their unique properties and identifies their potential for use.* Examines objects using the five senses to discover their properties and purposefully selects objects for use based on identified properties—e.g., when cleaning up a liquid spill, discards the piece of drawing paper initially used and selects a sponge for the purpose.

144

Key Content Ideas	*Performance Standards and Behavior Indicators*
MATTER (*continued*)	
Properties of objects can be changed by such forces as temperature, physical action, and mixing.	*Recognizes the relationship between forces that create the change and the results.* Experiments with and purposefully makes changes in the physical properties of objects, such as size, shape, color, and density—e.g., • adding more flour when the playdough becomes too wet. • squeezing the playdough to change its shape.
Collections of objects can be grouped and classified based on physical properties.	*Understands that objects can be grouped based on identical, similar, or related/class properties.* Spontaneously sorts and resorts collections of objects based on identical, similar, or related physical or functional properties—e.g., • collects, paper clips in one pile, irrespective of size. • collects the assorted tools for stamping in preparation for an art project.
Matter occurs in a solid, liquid, or gaseous state. Matter changes state when a force such as temperature.	*Identifies the differences between the solid, liquid, and gaseous states.* *Realizes that some matter changes state when a force such as heat is applied.* Purposefully makes changes in state using temperature and talks about what is happening—e.g., • Compares the state of a hardboiled egg to an uncooked egg, and talks about the difference as harder, with all the liquid gone. • Compares the way an ice cube melts to the way snow melts. • Requests to put orange juice in the freezer to make orange popsicles. • Talks about the way water disappears when it is left standing in a glass on the windowsill.

Key Content Ideas	Performance Standards and Behavior Indicators
PHYSICAL STRUCTURES	
The stability of a structure is influenced by the materials used and the design and balance of the construction.	*Understands that the stability of a structure is influenced by the materials used and the design and balance of the construction.* Experiments and purposefully seeks to control the stability of a structure through choice of material, balance, and design, such as enlarging the base of a structure or repositioning the blocks in different parts of the structure.
WATER	
Water flows down, unless acted upon by such forces as moving air, and such tools as pumps, waterwheels, and hoses.	*Realizes that the direction in which water flows can be controlled.* Experiments with and purposely seeks to control the movement of water using available tools.
Water takes the shape of the container it is in.	*Understands that water has no shape of its own.* Notices that water looks different in differently shaped containers and deliberately changes the shape of water by changing containers.
Water has surface tension (cohesion), as illustrated by the shape of a drop of water on a waxy or oiled surface.	*Realizes that water beads hold their shape and will continue to hold their shape when they are moved along a waxy surface.* Experiments with controlling the shape, size, and movement of water beads along different surfaces and talks about the water bead "having a skin" to hold it together.
Water adheres to other materials. (Adhesion) Materials vary in the amount of water they will absorb.	*Realizes that some materials absorb water and others do not.* *Recognizes that materials vary in the amount of water they will absorb.* Deliberately selects an absorbing material to wipe up liquid spills.

Key Content Ideas	Performance Standards and Behavior Indicators
WATER (*continued*)	
The buoyancy of an object depends upon its mass, weight, shape, and the density of the liquid in which it is placed.	*Begins to understand that mass, weight, and shape are the factors that determine whether an object floats, sinks, or is suspended in water or other types of liquids.* Experiments with floating and sinking and purposely selects objects that float or sink. Purposely alters one of the properties of an object to cause it to float or sink. Compares buoyancy of objects using different densities of liquid—e.g., oil and tomato juice.
Water mixes with some materials and not others. When water mixes with a material, usually the properties of all materials in the mixture change. Some changes can be reversed.	*Understands that materials vary in how they mix with water.* *Realizes that when water mixes with other materials all items in the mixture change in some way.* Purposefully selects materials for mixing with water and identifies the changes that occur to both the water and the material. Experiments with reversing changes—e.g., wetting and then drying clay.
MAGNETISM	
Magnetism is a force that attracts and repels.	*Understands that objects called magnets attract some objects and not others. Realizes that not all objects that look like metal are attracted by a magnet.* *Recognizes that magnets repel other magnets, but not other materials.* Sorts groups of objects based on whether the magnet picks them up or not. Begins to use the terms *magnetic, metal,* and *metallic-looking* when describing an object. Notices that some metals and metallic-looking objects are not magnetic.
The power of magnets varies and is not directly related to size.	*Realizes that magnets exert different amounts of force when attracting and holding objects.* *Realizes that the size of a magnet does not necessarily determine its power to attract.* Experiments and talks about the strength of different magnets. Demonstrates awareness that the size of a magnet does not determine its strength in attracting objects.

Key Content Ideas	Performance Standards and Behavior Indicators
MAGNETISM (*continued*)	
Magnetic force passes through such materials as air, water, paper, and some metallic objects, but not others.	*Realizes that magnets attract objects through air and such material barriers as paper and water.* Experiments with magnetic force with a variety of materials and talks about how the magnet attracts through some of them.
Magnets have a negative and positive pole. The closer the poles are together, the stronger the force.	*Realizes that a magnet can repel another magnet as well as attract it, but can't repel other objects.* Experiments with and talks about the repelling and attracting force between magnets.
Magnets have many uses in our daily life.	*Recognizes some of the ways we use magnets in our lives.* Purposefully selects a magnet for displaying work on a metal surface.
SOUND	
Sounds are produced by vibrations that result from different kinds of actions. Sounds travel from their source.	*Understands that sounds are produced by different events and are audible at various distances.* Experiments with producing and changing sounds by such actions as striking, shaking, rubbing objects together, or vocalizing, and talks about the differences. Locates the place of origin of sounds, both familiar and unfamiliar.
Sounds vary in volume, pitch, (high/low), quality, or resonance (squeaky, raspy).	*Distinguishes sounds in terms of volume, pitch, quality, and resonance, and relates them to the object producing the sound.* Labels familiar sounds. Identifies the object that is producing a familiar sound based on volume, pitch, quality, and resonance.
Sound patterns occur in music and language.	*Recognizes that sound patterns can be identified and produced in music and language.* Spontaneously sings, chants, and creates musical rhythms, rhymes, and other oral language patterns.
Sounds bounce off surfaces, as in echoes.	*Recognizes echoes as sounds that repeat from another source.* Experiments with initiating echoes.

Key Content Ideas	*Performance Standards and Behavior Indicators*
LIGHT	
Light comes from different sources. Under some conditions, a beam of light is visible and can be traced to its source.	*Recognizes that light comes from different sources.* Experiments with light beams using a flashlight and talks about the beam's direction.
Light can reflect off of some surfaces.	*Recognizes that light reflects off of some surfaces and not others.* Experiments with reflecting light using a mirror and other reflecting materials and describes observations.
Light can change color as it passes through different materials.	*Realizes that when light passes through some materials it changes color.* Discovers and experiments with "rainbow" effects when manipulating a light source.
SHADOWS	
A shadow is the darkness that is cast when light shines on an opaque object that is situated between a light source and a surface.	*Realizes that shadows are made by placing an opaque object between a light source and a surface.* Makes shadows by placing different materials in the space between the light source and a surface and identifies the object casting the shadow by looking at the shadow.
The shape of the shadow is determined by the shape and position of the object casting the shadow and the angle of the light in relation to the surface.	*Recognizes that the shape of a shadow can be changed by changing the object or its position in relationship to the light source and the surface.* Repeatedly changes the position of the object casting the shadow and talks about the changes in the shadow. Predicts changes in a shadow before changing the orientation
The size of a shadow changes when the distance between the light source and the object casting the shadow is changed.	*Realizes that the size of shadows can be changed by moving the object or light source.* Changes the size of the shadow by changing the distance between the object and the light source and explains the cause.

Key Content Ideas	Performance Standards and Behavior Indicators
MOVING AIR	
Moving air moves objects.	*Understands that moving air moves objects in a variety of ways.*
	Experiments with blowing objects with and without tools such as straws.
	Experiments with fanning the air to move objects.
Speed of movement of objects caused by moving air depends upon the speed and angle of air movement, the size and shape of the object, and the surface on which the object is moving.	*Realizes that the variables that affect the speed of movement of an object include intensity and direction of the force, the weight of the object, and the surfaces of both the moving object and the plane on which it is moving.*
	Changes force and direction when blowing through a straw to move objects.
	Deliberately seeks to control direction, speed, and distance of movement of an object by controlling the force of moving air—e.g., moving a cotton ball by blowing through a straw.
	Compares movement of different objects that are being moved by the same air force.
	Traces the path of movement of environmental objects after a windstorm.

APPENDIX B

Life Sciences Content

Key Content Ideas	Performance Standards and Behavior Indicators
PLANTS	
Plants' characteristics vary in structure and form, survival needs, and life cycles.	*Is aware of similarities and differences in characteristics of plants.*
There are similarities and differences in plants in terms of such characteristics as physical appearance, growth pattern, survival needs, and structure.	Describes and compares how plants look and grow, their structure, and what they need to survive.
The life cycle of plants include: germination, growth and change, reproduction and death. The stages in the life cycles of plants vary in form and duration.	*Recognizes that plants grow from seeds, and change as they grow. Recognizes that growing and changing events in the life cycle of plants are similar and different.*
	Observes, describes, and records changes as seeds sprout into seedlings and then grow into mature plants.
	Describes differences in time various seeds need to sprout.
The basic needs for plant survival generally include moisture, food, light, air, and space but vary in amount needed and in the way they obtain these essentials.	*Recognizes that plants have survival needs that include water, light, and temperature control.*
	Helps take care of plants and explains their needs for survival.
	Talks about similarities and differences in the survival needs of plants for water and light.

Key Content Ideas	Performance Standards and Behavior Indicators
ANIMALS	
Animals are classified into groups based on a variety of criteria. One set of criteria is the environment needed for survival: land, sea, or air.	*Realizes that animals can be grouped into different classes.* Distinguishes one group of animals from another by where they live: land, sea, or air.
The life cycle of animals include the following stages: birth, growth and development, reproduction, and death. Stages vary in duration.	*Recognizes developmental periods in animal life cycles.* Talks about differences in babies and adults in different species of animals. *Recognizes differences in timing and pacing of growth and change in different types of animals.* Compares the growth rates of various animals and people.
The body structures of animals vary and these structures determine the potential and limits of their patterns of living, such as movement and eating.	*Recognizes the relationship between the structure of an animal and the way it moves and eats.* Notices that the mouths of animals are different in size and shape and they pick up their food differently. Talks about how animals move differently and relates movement to body structure.
Animals vary in the kinds of habitats that they need.	*Recognizes the relationship between animal characteristics and their habitats.* Talks about people living in houses, fish living in the water, birds living in nests, and animals living in the ground or in various locations such as ant hills, and the reasons why.

Earth and Environmental Science Content

Key Content Ideas	Performance Standards and Behavior Indicators
WEATHER (in temperate climates)	
Weather changes seasonally in a predictable pattern that influences human and animal activity.	*Anticipates changes in activities relative to seasonal changes.* Talks about forthcoming activities when the weather changes, such as playing in the snow or going swimming. Identifies how people adapt the changing seasons. Notices changes in animal behavior, such as birds migrating when there are seasonal changes in temperature.
Seasonal changes affect the environment and plant world.	*Is aware of changes in the environment associated with seasonal changes.* Talks about the leaves falling from the trees and anticipates playing in leaf piles when the summer season ends. Notices that some trees do not lose leaves and asks questions about the differences.
Weather changes that influence human activity occur daily, sometimes with visible indicators.	*Recognizes some indicators of daily changes in weather and its relationship to human activity.* Anticipates rain when noticing dark clouds and talks about staying indoors.
ROCKS AND SOIL	
Soil and rocks make up a large part of the earth's surface. There are different kinds of rocks and soil.	*Recognizes that rocks vary in content, size, weight, and shape.* Sorts and resorts rocks and talks about similarities and differences. Experiments with rocks in water and sand, talks about differences in the way they interact in the two mediums. *Is aware that there are different kinds of soil.* Notices the difference between sand and conventional soil and uses them for different purposes.

Mathematics Content

Key Content Ideas	Performance Standards and Behavior Indicators
NUMBER AND OPERATIONS	

NCTM STANDARD: *Develops an understanding of numbers, ways to represent numbers, relationships among numbers, and the number system.* *

Number sense begins with (1) recognition of a set as a discrete collection, (2) identification of more, less, or the same quantity by matching one-to-one in correspondence between items in two different sets, (3) familiarity with the order of the names of counting numbers.	*Gains ability in the pre-counting skills: set recognition, matching items between sets in one-to-one correspondence, reciting of number words in order.* Creates and recreates sets of objects—e.g., attribute blocks, all round blocks, or all red blocks. Matches items between sets—e.g., one cylinder block on top of one unit block Recites or chants the number words in order without reference to objects or actions.
The counting numbers serve the purposes of specifying numerical quantity and sharing that information.	*Understands that the counting numbers serve a purpose in working with quantities.* Uses counting numbers in activities and identifies "how many" in sets of objects and actions based on counting. Uses number to make decisions about increasing and decreasing the number of items in a set.
Combining or partitioning (joining and separating) sets creates a new set of a different quantity. There is a consistent relationship between the quantity that is being joined or separated and the result (e.g., the addition of two items) consistently increases the quantity by the same numerical interval.	*Understands that quantities can be increased and decreased by joining and separating sets.* *Realizes that there is a predictable relationship in the change in numerical quantity through adding or removing items from sets.* Joins sets and counts the numerical quantity of the newly created set and then separates the set to recreate the two original sets, counting with each action. Retrieves additional items to complete a set—e.g., counts out 4 pegs to complete a pegboard row that has 4 spaces remaining. Uses interval counting when quantifying a set—e.g., counts 2 items at a time, 2,4,6, when counting a set.

Key Content Ideas	*Performance Standards and Behavior Indicators*
NUMBER AND OPERATIONS (*continued*)	
Numerical quantity can be represented in written form, as tallies, graphs, or numerals.	*Understands that numerical quantity can be represented in written form.* Uses tallies and written numerals to represent numerical quantities. Matches written numerals to sets of the same.
GEOMETRY	

NCTM STANDARDS: *Develops an understanding of shape geometry that deals with the attributes of two- and three-dimensional figures. Develops an understanding of locational geometry that deals with location/position in terms of spatial relationships.* *

Geometric shapes have unique properties and characteristics that distinguish them from one another.	*Distinguishes two- and three-dimensional geometric shapes by their unique properties and characteristics.* Names, matches, and identifies geometric shapes in the environment. Uses a variety of materials to create and re-create 2-D and 3-D geometric shapes using spatial memory and visualization. Solves puzzles using shapes by turning and flipping the pieces. Describes simple geometric shapes (circle, triangle, rectangle, and square) and indicates their position in relation to self and other objects. Investigates and predicts results of putting together and taking apart two- and three-dimensional shapes.
The location of an object on a surface or in space is determined by its relationship to other points in the same area.	*Recognizes that the location of an object is always defined by its relationship to another object.* Uses location language such as "near," "next to," "on top of," "at the corner" to find and describe position in space. Interprets relative positions in space, such as nearer and farther away. Describes, names, and interprets direction and distance in navigating space and applies ideas about direction and distance.

Key Content Ideas	*Performance Standards and Behavior Indicators*
MEASUREMENT	

NCTM STANDARD: *Measurement is a way to describe physical properties of objects, surface areas, and distances in space, and to specify locations.* *

Key Content Ideas	*Performance Standards and Behavior Indicators*
Physical properties of objects can be measured and compared using nonstandard and/or standard units.	*Understands the measurable attributes of objects and ways to measure them.* Talks about the attributes of length, volume, weight, surface area, and temperature, and uses non-standard and standard units to measure these attributes—e.g., "longer-shorter," "2 unit blocks long," "one foot long." Compares and orders objects according to these attributes.
Distances can be measured and compared using non-standard and/or standard units.	*Understands that the measurement of distance is obtained by using non-standard and standard tools.* Purposefully selects and uses non-standard and standard tools to measure distances—e.g., five footsteps to door; three feet from the floor.
ALGEBRA	

NCTM STANDARD: *Recognizes patterns of relationships, uses symbols to represent patterns and mathematical situations, and makes models of quantitative relationships.* *

Key Content Ideas	*Performance Standards and Behavior Indicators*
A set is a collection of objects, events, or ideas that are grouped and regrouped for a reason.	*Independently groups and regroups a set of objects and events based on a common physical property or a classification schema.* Sorts sets of objects—such as vehicles—by physical properties such as color or class. Sorts events by attributes, such as intensity of sound.
Patterning is a way of establishing order within a set and between sets.	*Creates patterns within sets of objects/events using a repeated unit and explains the basis for the pattern.* Patterns objects/events in a set in increasingly complex ways—e.g., • single alternation: "red, blue" or "loud, soft sounds" • double alternation: "red, red, blue, blue" • 2-1 pattern: "red, red, blue" • 1-3-1 pattern: "red, blue, blue, blue, red" Labels the pattern based on the unit that defines the pattern—e.g., a "triangle-circle" or "triangle, triangle, circle" pattern. Makes predictions of what comes next in a sequence based on observed patterns.

Key Content Ideas	*Performance Standards and Behavior Indicators*
DATA ANALYSIS AND PROBABILITY	

NCTM STANDARD: *Formulates questions that can be addressed with data and collects, organizes, and displays relevant data to answer them.* *

	Collects information to answer questions of interest and records the information in a way that can be retrieved, analyzed, and shared.
Information in the form of data can be collected, recorded, analyzed, and displayed.	Formulates questions, collects and records answers, and summarizes findings.
	Shares recorded information with others and interprets the findings—e.g., "More people like chocolate ice cream so we should buy more chocolate than vanilla."
	Compares data from different sources, such as more people in this class like to use magnets than in the other class.

*All Standards are based on NCTM, 2000.

APPENDIX E

Social Studies Content

Purpose: The primary purpose of the social studies is to help young people develop the ability to make informed and reasoned decisions for the public good as citizens of a culturally diverse, democratic society and an interdependent world (National Council for the Social Studies, 2004, p. 40).

Subject areas in Social Studies include Anthropology, Archaeology, Economics,* Geography,* History,* Philosophy, Political Science, Psychology,* Religion, Sociology,* Humanities.

*Subjects outlined in this content summary

Key Content Ideas	Performance Standards and Behavior Indicators
SOCIOLOGY AND PSYCHOLOGY	
A major attribute of a democratic society is that policies and rules are made by members of the society in order to balance the rights of individuals with the rights of a group.	*Understands the importance of being a responsible member of a group and the standards necessary for a group to function successfully.* Helps formulate and follow class rules. Talks about *fairness* of rules and the need for rules—e.g., setting limits on size of groups in interest centers.
Members of a group have common and unique needs and have similar and different perspectives.	*Recognizes and respects similarities and differences in perspectives and needs among members of the group in order to meet common needs.* Shares and cooperates with others. Communicates feelings, preferences, views, and ideas. Expresses caring and respect for the feelings and ideas of others.

Key Content Ideas	*Performance Standards and Behavior Indicators*
SOCIOLOGY AND PSYCHOLOGY (*continued*)	
Members of a group have similar and different talents and abilities needed by the community.	*Realizes that peers and adults vary in their abilities and talents to contribute to the community in which they are a member.* Recognizes and calls upon talents of peers in curriculum and routine events. Volunteers to use own talents to contribute to classroom activities.
Roles and functions in a business or service community are defined in order to fulfill the intended purpose.	*Identifies needed roles to be fulfilled and who fulfills them within the class and the larger community.* Volunteers to help perform various responsibilities in the classroom. Helps monitor the job assignments in the classroom. Identifies and describes roles in a business or service community.
HISTORY	
Historical events follow a time line based on a progression from past events, to present events and leading to future events. Past events affect current events and current decisions affect future events.	*Demonstrates increasing awareness of the relationship between events in time sequences within each day and between yesterday (days in the past), today, and tomorrow (days in the future).* Identifies daily and weekly event sequences and the results of changes in these sequences, such as results of changes in schedule, emerging needs for new rules.
GEOGRAPHY	
People live in communities that are bounded by geographic areas. Facilities within a community meet the needs of the community—e.g., homes, businesses, educational, religious, and recreational facilities.	*Is aware that communities are bounded by geographic/space factors that influence their lives in both indoor and outdoor community areas.* Makes simple 3-D maps of familiar areas that define an indoor or outdoor space (classroom, home, post office, police/fire station, park).

Key Content Ideas	Performance Standards and Behavior Indicators
GEOGRAPHY (*continued*)	
Communities have pathways that facilitate moving between primary facilities. 2-D and 3-D maps are representations of land use of physical space.	*Understands the difference between different kinds of pathways in a community.* Makes simple 3-D and 2-D maps that distinguish people and vehicle pathways between familiar facilities in the neighborhood—e.g., bridges, train tracks, sidewalks, roadways.
ECONOMICS	
People produce goods and services, and provide them in exchange for some form of payment—either money or equally valued goods or services.	*Demonstrates awareness of the need to make equivalent exchanges for objects and services with materials or money.* Talks about the different kinds of skills required to fulfill various roles. Dramatizes the exchange of goods and services for money or other goods and services.
People earn money by fulfilling needed roles in a community using unique skills that are required in the role. Money is a common means of exchange for goods and services.	*Realizes that the different job roles require different skills and meet the needs of a community.* Dramatizes job roles in different kinds of service communities—e.g., putting out a fire.
There is a relationship between supply and demand.	*Realizes that there are not always enough resources to meet the demand.* Understands that it is necessary to take turns with materials when there is not enough for everybody to use at once.

Language and Literacy Content

- The function of language is to communicate.
- Communication requires using a common language to receive, transmit, and exchange messages for information and understanding, literacy response and expression, critical analysis, and evaluation and social interaction.
- Communication as it relates to literacy occurs in oral, graphic, symbolic, and print forms.

Key Content Ideas	Performance Standards and Behavior Indicators
ORAL COMMUNICATION: Listening and Speaking	
Oral language is a universal form of communication between and among people, in terms of receiving and giving messages. In order to effectively communicate messages through oral language there needs to be common agreement on the meanings of the language.	*Understands that communication involves listening and speaking for different purposes.* Shares ideas, opinions, and perceptions of personal experience; communicates wishes and feelings, requests information. Listens with understanding to conversations, directions, rhymes, stories. Understands and follows simple and multistep directions.
The more precise the language, the more effective the communication is likely to be. Words vary in meaning to different people and under different circumstances.	*Expands vocabulary and uses more complex language to communicate.* Incorporates new words into spoken vocabulary. Is increasingly more precise in descriptions of experiences and for requests.

Key Content Ideas	*Performance Standards and Behavior Indicators*
ORAL COMMUNICATION: Listening and Speaking (*continued*)	
Spoken messages are influenced by intonation, pacing, and gestures. Words and actions don't always carry the same message.	*Understands that differences in tone, body language, and pacing affect the meaning of messages people receive.* Uses actions to help transmit a message when needed and observes actions of others when receiving a message. Changes pace or speech when speaking with second-language learners.
Phonological awareness is the ability to discriminate and identify sounds in spoken language.	*Recognizes rhyming words and similar beginning sounds in spoken language, chants and song.* Matches rhymes and makes up rhymes. Matches and makes up alliterative sounds connected to oral language.
WRITTEN COMMUNICATION: Reading and Writing	
Written language represents spoken language. People write to transform spoken language to written language and read to transform written language to spoken language.	*Makes connections between oral and written language.* Reads and draws signs in context—e.g., reads traffic signs and job charts. Writes some text—e.g., writes shopping list for class party, labels art products and block constructions; writes simple sentences to describe experiences or tell a story. Reads some text—e.g., activities listed on a daily class schedule, instructions for a cooking activity, a simple repetitive story. Makes connections between written words and the letter sounds involved in reading.

Key Content Ideas	Performance Standards and Behavior Indicators
WRITTEN COMMUNICATION: Reading and Writing (*continued*)	
The more standard the form of written communication, the more universally available is the message. There are a standard set of rules that govern written communication.	*Realizes that concepts of print are used in both reading and writing.* When writing, uses concepts of print–e.g., directionality from left to right, spacing between words, and punctuation. Reads environmental print and understands the meanings in terms of action–e.g., "exit," "job chart." Reads familiar stories.
Recorded communications are permanent resources, providing opportunities for revisiting to validate information, and obtain increased meaning.	*Understands that writing is a permanent record that can be revisited.* *Understands the need to use different forms of recording for different purposes, such as drawing, charts, conventional writing.* Demonstrates an increase in understanding of and appreciation for written material by seeking more opportunities to read and write. Revisits books to obtain information.

Guide for Planning and Implementing Themes

Selecting a Topic

- Observe and listen to children in order to identify interests that might be suitable for a focused set of curriculum activities.
- Consider the following questions in order to make a selection:
  - Does the topic allow for in-classroom exploration?
  - Does the topic invite children to connect new experiences with their prior knowledge?
  - Is the topic one that interests you as a teacher?
  - Is it one that you will be able to pursue?
  - Are adequate materials and community resources available?

Key Content Ideas and Facts Associated with the Topic

- Make a list of key ideas that children can begin to develop related to the topic. Use a variety of resources (e.g., literature, computer, community members, colleagues, parents).
- Identify the facts related to the ideas that children can acquire through action-based activities and can be connected to their prior knowledge.
- Make a list of important vocabulary words and terms to be used with children as the topic develops.

Planning a Launch Activity

- Identify several possibilities for initially engaging the children's interest, e.g., read-aloud, introduction of a new set of materials, a new experience, and a trip.
- Make a selection from the possibilities based on observations of the way you have observed the children pursue and develop interests.
- Identify performance standards this activity will address and plan for assessment.

Planning for Collecting Information by Children Related to the Topic

- Introduce new materials related to the topic for children to examine and discuss during *meeting time.*
- Use *read-alouds* and *shared reading experiences* to stimulate children's acquisition of new information and making connections with prior understandings.
- Where appropriate, list potential *music/movement/gross motor activities* that can contribute to children's understanding of the topic.
- Identify performance standards and behavior indicators that these activities will address and plan for assessment.

Plan Small Group and Independent Activities in Centers

- Design teacher-planned small-group activities to contribute to children's increasing understanding of key ideas associated with the topic.
- Collect materials and resources to add to centers to stimulate children's pursuit of content understandings related to the topic.
- Identify performance standards and behavior indicators these activities will address and plan for assessment.

Planning a Culminating Activity/Event

- Plan with children to design an event that will summarize and celebrate what they have learned related to the topic.
- Plan ways to review with children and document their understandings of the key concepts and facts that helped them better understand the topic.
- Plan for ways to communicate to parents, colleagues, and other classroom visitors how this activity addresses local Assessment of Performance Standards and Behavior Indicators.

Focused Curriculum Planning Form

Focus/Theme/Topic: _____

Key Concepts
Key Vocabulary

Activity Plans	Performance Standard and Behavior Indicator
GROUP TIME	
Launch Activities:	
Follow-up Activities:	
Read-Alouds and Shared Reading:	
Music/Gross Motor Activities:	
CENTER TIME	
Independent Center Activities:	
Adult-Designed Center Activities:	
CULMINATING ACTIVITY	
Celebrating by sharing with family, other classes, and interested adults.	

Sample Theme: Shoes

Key Content Ideas
• Shoes serve a function, e.g., protection, sports, decoration.
• Shoes have common properties, e.g., soles, method of keeping on feet, come in pairs.
• Shoes vary in color, shape, size, materials, and construction.
• Cultural groups vary in preference for shoe styles.
• Shoes are manufactured either by machine or by hand.
• Other forms of footwear include boots, clods, flip-flops, ice skates, roller skates.
• Weather conditions affect choice of footwear.
Key Vocabulary
Shoe characteristics: sole, tongue, toe, heel, lace, buckle, strap, leather, canvas, suede, stitching, pair, size
Care of shoes: shoemaker, cobbler, Brannock (shoe-measuring device), shoe horn, shoe trees
Environmental conditions: hot, warm, cold, snowy, icy, rainy, muddy
Cultural groups: Alaskan natives, Chinese, Native Americans, Dutch, Hawaiian

GROUP TIME	
Activity Plans	*Performance Standard and Behavior Indicator*
Launch Activity possibilities	*Literacy and Music*
Literature Entry: Poem or book	*Listens and speaks for different purposes.*
Talk Entry: Teacher's or children's personal tales	
Object/Artifact Entry:	Shares ideas, opinions, and perceptions of personal experience.
• Shoe box	
• Unfamiliar shoe style: "Have you ever seen a box/shoe like this before?"	Responds orally and in action to music.
Music Entry: Song, instrumental, dance	

---

*Adapted from CUNY Literacy Project *Shoe Unit* (1999), York College, Guy Brewer Blvd., Jamaica, N.Y. (unpublished)

Follow-up Activity possibilities • Put shoes in a communal pile and sort. • Record data using pictures related to children's shoe colors or types. • Compare two different shoes for similarities and differences–record information on a graphic organizer. • Compare shoe sizes. • Organize shoes in size order. • Group discussion–"If we were going to make a shoe, what would we need? What would we do?"	*Literacy and Mathematics* Sorts based on physical properties and explains the reason. Records information. Uses measurement strategies to compare size and length.
Read-Alouds and Shared Reading Poems Theme books (See Shoe Theme book list on p. 184)	*Literacy* Listens with understanding to conversations, rhymes, stories.
Music/Gross Motor Activities • Make sound patterns with shoes. • Contrast sounds of various shoes on different surfaces. • Mimic walking wearing different types of shoes.	*Creative Expression* Copies a model and initiates patterns of musical sounds and actions in response to music.

Center Time	*Performance Standard and Behavior Indicator*
Independent Center Activities: • Shoe store or shoe repair shop in dramatic center. • Sole prints at art center. • Shoe collage using magazine/newspaper pictures. • Sole prints in sand table. • Seriate shoes by size. • Match shoes to sole cutouts. • Match shoes by touch.	
Adult-Designed Center Activities: • Tell a tale to a small group and involve children in changing the shoes on flannel board figure to conform to weather in the story situations. • Construct "shoes" using a wide variety of construction and art materials. • Take children's dictation related to their writing/ drawing about favorite shoes.	
Culminating Activity • Write a class story or book about the class experiences while pursuing the shoe theme. • Set up an annotated picture display/document panel with photos of children involved in theme activities and samples of the products they produced.	

Developmental Continuum for Visual Discrimination

Entry Level

Object to Object:

*   Match identical objects in environment using concrete, real, and representational objects.
*   Match identical geometric shapes, sort and compare similar shapes, and classify related shapes using attribute blocks, pattern blocks, and other appropriate manipulatives.

Object to Picture:

*   Match concrete object to picture of object, such as matching blocks to labels of blocks.
*   Match concrete shapes to picture of shapes, such as matching tangrams and pattern blocks to pictures.

Picture to Picture:

*   Match picture of representational object to picture, such as animal or food lotto games.
*   Match pictures of shapes to other pictures of shapes, such as shape lotto.

Higher Level

Lines and Curves:

*   Compare, match, and identify a variety of straight lines and open and closed curves using concrete materials such as pipe cleaners, clay, yarn, sticks, etc. Compare straight and curved lines in positional relationships (next to, above, below, higher, lower, etc.) using concrete objects.

Letters:

*   Match identical letters (alphabet puzzles, magnet letters, etc.)
*   Match similar letters (magazines, environmental print)
*   Match letter clusters (name cards, environmental print such as "exit, stop")

Linking Visual to Language

*   Respond to request to find named letters. ("I need an 'A,' please find one for me?")
*   Verbally identify letters by name. (This is a "B.")
*   Verbally identify letter clusters (names, environmental print).

Developmental Continuum for Auditory Discrimination

Level I (entry)—Classroom and Environmental Sounds

- Match grossly different sounds made by concrete objects that are visible in the environment.
- Match, sort, classify, and discriminate between sounds with increasingly finer differences—e.g., bells representing a musical scale.
- Identify familiar outdoor sounds by listening to tape recordings of the sounds.

Level II (advanced level)—Sounds of Language (Phonological Awareness)

Rhyming:

1. Repeat rhymes.
2. Identify rhymes through physical response (e.g., clapping, snapping fingers).
3. Identify rhymes by filling in missing rhyme in rhyme pairs.
4. Create rhymes, including nonsense rhymes.

Syllabication:

Identify the sound units in words through activities such as clapping, tapping, or counting syllables in words.

Progress from familiar to unfamiliar words (children's names to new words).

Phonemic Awareness

Alliteration:

1. Repeat initial sounds or phonemes in word context.
2. Identify identical initial sounds with a physical response.
3. Create a series of alliterative words and/or nonsense words.

Sound Substitution:

Initial word sounds: Playfully substitute one initial sound in a familiar word for another, such as the song "Willoughby, Wallaby, Woo," or changing "Wee Willie Winkle" to "Dee Dillie Dinkle."

Segmenting of Phonemes:

Orally breaking down a word into individual phonemes.

Blending of Phonemes:

Listening to a group of phonemes and orally blending them into a word.

Phonics (Highest Level)

Linking phonemes with the alphabetic principle to decode written words.

Developmental Continuum for Developing Number Sense

Making and organizing sets: The learnings children need to develop before counting.

Grouping and sorting based on:

1. Personal reasons, without observable properties in common; e.g., "my toys"
2. Identical physical properties such as color, shape
3. Similar physical properties, such as multiple sizes of one shape
4. Similar functions, such as "vehicles that roll"

Contexts:

- *Using concrete materials:* varied collections of high-interest materials that are already available, such as mixed collections of blocks, miniature people and vehicles, and materials collections that have been purposefully selected, such as buttons.
- *Producing actions,* such as jumping and skipping
- *Making sounds,* such as clapping and stamping

Ordering and patterning objects in a set:

1. Clustering, piling, bunching, arranging in rows or lines
2. Copying, extending, creating patterns with repeated units:

AB AB AB	Red-Blue, Red-Blue, Red-Blue
AABB AABB	☺☺☹☹ ☺☺☹☹
ABC ABC ABC	☺☺☹ ☺☺☹ ☺☺☹
ABB ABB ABB	☺☹☹ ☺☹☹ ☺☹☹

3. Placing objects in a serial order based on a property, such as longest to shortest, biggest to smallest.

Quantifying sets or collections:

- After experiences with creating and organizing sets, children begin to think in terms of counting and quantifying.
- Describing quantity of collections using non-numerical terms, such as "a lot," "some," "many"
- Comparing quantity of two different collections, using non-numerical terms such as "more than," "less than"
- Using number to quantify

Note: successful counting depends upon the development of the following subskills that are acquired in a variety of experiences prior to counting.

1. 1-1 Correspondence—setting table
2. Familiarity with the names of the numbers in order—1, 2, 3
3. Awareness of the boundaries of a set that is being counted—i.e., the amount of items to be counted

Each of the subskills is required in order to count successfully. When counting breaks down, it is important to note which subskill is actually breaking down in order to plan experiences in a noncounting activity that will strengthen that subskill.

Before children use written numerals to describe or represent the size of the set, they use other ways to represent a set.

Representing Sets

- *using pictures,* such as flannel board cutouts to represent the three bears
- *using other objects,* such as chips, to represent the number of children in the group
- *tallying,* such as making Xs for recording children's preferences, e.g., ice cream flavors
- *reading (naming) and writing numerals (order is not important)*
- *connecting numerals to sets of that size*

Mathematics Observation Recording Form

CHILD'S NAME_____

Naturally Occurring Event		*Teacher-Designed Activities*	
NUMBER			
Understand numbers, ways of representing numbers, relationships among numbers, and number systems			
Uses counting numbers in activities and recognizes "how many" in sets of objects based on counting.			
Date	Specify the level of quantification	Date	Specify the level of quantification
Connects numerals to the quantities they represent, using various physical models and representations.			
Date	Specify the level of quantification	Date	Specify the level of quantification

Naturally Occurring Event		*Teacher-Designed Activities*	
GEOMETRY			
Analyze characteristics and properties of two- and three-dimensional geometric shapes and develop mathematical arguments about geometric relationships.			
Recognizes geometric shapes in the environment by marching and labeling.			
Date	Specify shapes and context	Date	Specify shapes and context
Sorts two- and three-dimensional shapes			
Date	Specify materials used	Date	Specify materials used
Finds and names locations with simple relationships such as "near to"			
Date	Specify labels used	Date	Specify labels used
MEASUREMENT			
Understand measurable attributes of objects.			
Recognizes the attributes of length, volume, weight.			
Date	Specify the measures and materials used	Date	Specify the measures and materials used
Compares and orders objects according to measurement attributes.			
Date	Specify the attribute and materials used	Date	Specify the attribute and materials used

Naturally Occurring Event		***Teacher-Designed Activities***	
MEASUREMENT (*continued*)			
Uses non-standard units to measure.			
Date	Specify units used and objects measured	Date	Specify units used and objects measured
Uses standard units to measure.			
Date	Specify units used and objects measured	Date	Specify units used and objects measured
ALGEBRA			
Understand patterns. *Sorts, classifies, and orders objects by size, number, and other properties, and translates from one representation to another.*			
Recognizes, describes, and extends patterns such as sequences of sounds and shapes or simple number.			
Date	Specify pattern and context	Date	Specify pattern and context
Analyze change in various contexts.			
Describes quantitative change, such as explaining a change in the height of a plant using some kind of measurement unit.			
Date	Specify the change and context	Date	Specify the change and context

Physical Science Observation Recording Form

CHILD'S NAME: _____

	Naturally Occurring Event	*Date*	*Teacher-Designed Activity*	*Date*
Observes and talks about physical properties of objects	Specify: objects and properties		Specify: objects and properties	
Compares and contrasts properties of objects	Specify: objects and properties		Specify: objects and properties	
Notices and talks about and compares changes in properties in interaction events	Specify: materials and changes		Specify: materials and changes	
Predicts changes in properties and/or behavior of objects during events: e.g., magnets, buoyancy, absorbency, texture, balance	Specify: materials, prediction, changes		Specify: materials, predictions, changes	
Experiments: tests and retest results Force and movement of objects	Specify: materials and experiments		Specify: materials and experiments	
Experiments with properties of water	Specify: properties being tested		Specify: properties being tested	
Experiments with properties of sound	Specify: properties being tested		Specify: properties being tested	
Experiments with properties of light	Specify: properties being tested		Specify: properties being tested	

Sample Checklist:
Alphabetic Knowledge

CHILD'S NAME: _____

Dates: Oct: _____   **Jan-Feb:** _____   **May:** _____

Level	Naturally Occurring Event: Circle letters	Teacher-Designed Task: Circle letters	Adult Notes
Matches identical concrete letters	a b c d e f g h i j k l m n o p q r s t u v w x y z A B C D E F G H I J K L M N O P Q R S T U V W X Y Z	a b c d e f g h i j k l m n o p q r s t u v w x y z A B C D E F G H I J K L M N O P Q R S T U V W X Y Z	
Matches identical written letters	a b c d e f g h i j k l m n o p q r s t u v w x y z A B C D E F G H I J K L M N O P Q R S T U V W X Y Z	a b c d e f g h i j k l m n o p q r s t u v w x y z A B C D E F G H I J K L M N O P Q R S T U V W X Y Z	
Matches letter clusters; e.g., names, environmental print	LIST	LIST	
Responds to request to find named letters	a b c d e f g h i j k l m n o p q r s t u v w x y z A B C D E F G H I J K L M N O P Q R S T U V W X Y Z	a b c d e f g h i j k l m n o p q r s t u v w x y z A B C D E F G H I J K L M N O P Q R S T U V W X Y Z	
Verbally identifies letters by name	a b c d e f g h i j k l m n o p q r s t u v w x y z A B C D E F G H I J K L M N O P Q R S T U V W X Y Z	a b c d e f g h i j k l m n o p q r s t u v w x y z A B C D E F G H I J K L M N O P Q R S T U V W X Y Z	
Verbally identifies letter clusters	LIST	LIST	

Visual Discrimination
Observation Recording Form

Child's Name: _____

Level of Matching and Grouping	Naturally Occurring Activity	Teacher-Designed Activity
OBJECT TO OBJECT		
	Date:	Date:
Identical representational objects in the environment—e.g., dolls, dishes, straws.		
Similar and related representational objects—e.g., collections of fruit, miniature cars		
Identical concrete geometric shape—e.g., same size and color triangles		
Similar and *related* concrete geometric shapes—e.g., different types of triangles		
OBJECT TO PICTURE		
Concrete objects to pictures of the objects—e.g., car to car		
Geometric shapes to pictures of the shapes—e.g., squares to squares		
PICTURE TO PICTURE		
Picture of object to picture of object—e.g., in such activities as lotto and memory games		
Picture of geometric shape to picture of geometric shape—e.g., shape lotto, shape dominoes		
LOCATIONAL TERMS		
Identify positions and locations of objects in the environment—e.g., next to, above, below		
Identify positions and locations of pictured objects in magazines and books—e.g., next to, above, below.		

References

Almy, M., & Genishi, C. (1979). *Ways of studying children.* New York: Teachers College Press.

Althouse, R., Johnson, M. H., & Mitchell, S. T. (2003). *The colors of learning: Integrating the visual arts into the early childhood curriculum.* New York: Teachers College Press.

Arnheim, R. (1969). *Visual thinking.* London: Faber and Faber.

Bartlett, F. (1969). Art: Representation and expression. In M. Brearley (Ed.), *The teaching of young children: Some implications of Piaget's learning theory* (pp. 34–51). New York: Shocken Books.

Beaty, J. (1986). *Observing development of the young child.* Columbus, OH: Merrill.

Beaty, J., & Pratt, L. (2007). *Early literacy in preschool and kindergarten: A multicultural perspective* (2nd ed.). Upper Saddle River, NJ: Pearson Education.

Becker, W., Engelmann, S., & Rhine, W. (1981). Direct instruction model. In W. Rhine (Ed.), *Making schools more effective: New directions from Follow Through* (pp. 95–154). New York: Academic Press.

Biggs, R. (1990). *The snowman storybook.* New York: Random House.

Boehm, A., & Weinberg, R. (1996). *The classroom observer: Developing observation skills in early childhood settings* (3rd ed.). New York: Teachers College Press.

Brearley, M. (1970). *The teaching of young children: Some implications of Piaget's learning theory.* New York: Schocken.

Bredekamp, S. (Ed.). (1987). *Position statement on standardized testing of young children 3 through 8 years of age.* Washington, DC: National Association for the Education of Young Children.

Bredekamp, S., & Copple, C. (Eds.). (2009). *Developmentally appropriate practice in early childhood programs.* Washington, DC: National Association for the Education of Young Children.

Bredekamp, S., & Rosegrant, T. (Eds.). (1992). *Reaching potentials: Appropriate curriculum and assessment for young children* (Vol. 1). Washington, DC: National Association for the Education of Young Children.

Carle, E. (1990). *Pancakes, pancakes.* New York: Scholastic.

Carpenter, T., Fennema, E., Franke, M., Levi, L., & Empson, S. (1999). *Children's mathematics: Cognitively guided instruction.* Portsmouth, NH: Heinemann.

Chalufour, I., & Worth, K. (2004). *Building structures with young children.* St. Paul, MN: Redleaf Press.

Chalufour, I., & Worth, K. (2005). *Exploring water with young children.* St. Paul, MN: Redleaf Press.

Chukovsky, K. (1968). *From two to five.* Berkeley: University of California Press.

Clay, M. (1991). *Becoming literate: The construction of inner control.* Portsmouth, NH: Heinemann.

Clements, D. (1999). Geometric and spatial thinking in young children. In J. Copley (Ed.), *Mathematics in the early years* (pp. 66–79). Washington, DC: National Association for the Education of Young Children and National Council of Teachers of Mathematics.

Cohen, D., Stern, V., & Balaban, N. (2008). *Observing and recording the behavior of young children* (5th ed.). New York: Teachers College Press.

Colker, L. (2005). *The cooking book: Fostering young children's learning and delight.* Washington, DC: National Association for the Education of Young Children.

Cornett, C. (1998). *The arts as meaning makers.* Upper Saddle River, NJ: Prentice Hall.

Cuffaro, H. (1995). *Experimenting with the world: John Dewey and the early childhood classroom.* New York: Teachers College Press.

Dewey, J. (1902). *The child and the curriculum and The school and society.* Chicago: University of Chicago Press.

Dewey, J. (1963). *Experience and education.* New York: Collier. (Original work published 1938)

Dittmann, L. (Ed.). (1970). *Curriculum is what happens: Planning is the key.* Washington, DC: National Association for the Education of Young Children.

Dodds, A. (1996). *The shape of things.* Cambridge, MA: Candlewick Press.

Dodge, T. D., & Colker, L. (1992). *The creative curriculum for early childhood* (3rd ed.). Washington, DC: Teaching Strategies.

Donaldson, M. (1978). *Children's minds.* London: Fontana and New York: Norton.

Douglas, K., & Jaquith, D. (2009). *Engaging learners through artmaking: Choice-based art education in the classroom.* New York: Teachers College Press.

Eisner, E. (1990). The role of art and play in children's cognitive development. In E. Klugman & S. Smilansky (Eds.), *Children's play and learning: Perspectives and policy implications* (pp. 43–57). New York: Teachers College Press.

Elkind, D. (1990). Academic pressure—"Too much too soon: The demise of play." In E. Klugman & S. Smilansky (Eds.), *Children's play and learning: Perspectives and policy implications* (pp. 3–17). New York: Teachers College Press.

Epstein, A. (2007). *The intentional teacher: Choosing the best strategies for young children's learning.* Washington, DC: National Association for the Education of Young Children.

Erikson, E. (1972). Play and actuality. In M. Piers (Ed.), *Play and development: A symposium* (pp. 127–167). New York: Norton.

Falk, B. (2009). *Teaching the way children learn.* New York: Teachers College Press.

Ferreiro, E., & Teberosky, A. (1982). *Literacy before schooling.* Portsmouth, NH: Heinemann.

Forman, G., & Kuschner, D. (1983). *The child's construction of knowledge.* Washington, DC: National Association for the Education of Young Children.

Fromberg, D. (1995). *The full-day kindergarten: Planning and practicing a dynamic themes curriculum* (2nd ed.). New York: Teachers College Press.

Garrison, J. (1979). *Child arts: Integrating curriculum through the arts.* Menlo Park, CA: Addison-Wesley.

Genishi, C. (Ed.). (1992). *Ways of assessing children and curriculum: Stories of early childhood practice.* New York: Teachers College Press.

Gersten, R., Darch, C., & Gleason, M. (1988). Effectiveness of direct instruction academic kindergarten for children from low income families. *The Elementary School Journal, 89*(2), 226–240.

Gibran, K. (1923). *The prophet.* New York: Knopf.

Ginsberg, H., Inoue, N., & Seo, K. (2008). Young children doing mathematics: Observations of everyday activities. In J. Copley (Ed.), *Mathematics in the early years* (pp. 88–100). Washington, DC: National Association of Early Childhood Education & National Council of Teachers of Mathematics.

Goffin, S., & Wilson, C. (2001). *Curriculum models in early childhood education: Appraising the relationship* (2nd ed.). Upper Saddle River, NJ: Prentice Hall.

Good, R. (1977). *How children learn science: Conceptual development and implications for teaching.* New York: Macmillan.

Good, T., & Brophy, J. (2008). *Looking in classrooms* (10th ed.). Boston: Allyn and Bacon.

Greene, R. (2001). *When a line bends—A shape begins.* Boston: Houghton Mifflin.

Gronlund, G. (2006). *Making early learning standards come alive: Connecting your practice and curriculum to state guidelines.* St. Paul, MN: Redleaf Press.

Halliday, M. (1973). *Explorations in the functions of language.* London: Edward Arnold.

Harlen, J. (1992). *Science experiences for the early childhood years* (5th ed.). New York: Macmillan.

Harste, J., Woodward, V., & Burke, C. (1984). *Language stories and literacy lessons.* Portsmouth, NH: Heinemann.

Hartley, R., Frank, L., & Goldenson, R. (1952). *Understanding children's play.* New York: Columbia University Press.

Helm, J., & Beneke, S. (Eds.). (2003). *The power of projects: Meeting contemporary challenges in early childhood classrooms—strategies and solutions.* New York: Teachers College Press.

High Scope Educational Foundation. (2003). *Child observation record.* Ypsilanti, MI: High Scope Press.

Hill, D. (1977). *Mud, sand and water.* Washington, DC: National Association for the Education of Young Children.

Hirsch, E. (Ed.). (1974). *The block book.* Washington, DC: National Association for the Education of Young Children.

Hohmann, M., & Weikart, D. (1995). *Educating young children: Active learning activities in preschool and child care programs.* Ypsilanti, MI: High Scope Press.

Jablon, J., Dombro, A., & Dichtelmiller, M. (2007). *The power of observation* (2nd ed.). Washington, DC: National Association for the Education of Young Children and Teaching Strategies.

Johnson, H. (1933). *The art of block building.* New York: Bank Street College of Education.

Jones, E., & Reynolds, G. (1992). *The play's the thing: Teacher roles in children's play.* New York: Teachers College Press.

Kamii, C. (2000). *Number in preschool and kindergarten.* Washington, DC: National Association for the Education of Young Children.

Katz, L., & Chard, S. (2000). *Engaging children's minds: The project approach* (2nd ed.). Greenwich, CT: Ablex.

Klugman, E., & Smilansky, S. (Eds.). (1990). *Children's play and learning: Perspectives and policy implications.* New York: Teachers College Press.

Kohn, A. (2001, September). Five reasons to stop saying "good job." *Young Children, 56*(5), 24–29.

Koplow, L. (Ed.). (1996). *Unsmiling faces: How preschools can heal.* New York: Teachers College Press.

Kostelnik, M., Soderman, A., & Whiren, A. (2007). *Developmentally appropriate curriculum: Best practices in early childhood education* (4th ed.). Upper Saddle River, NJ: Pearson Education.

Lowenfeld, M. (1967). *Play in childhood*. New York: John Wiley and Sons.

Lowenfeld, V. (1957). *Creative and mental growth* (3rd ed.). New York: John Wiley and Sons.

Malcolm, S. (1998). Making sense of the world. In *Dialogue on early childhood science, mathematics and technology education* (Project 2061, pp. 8–13). Washington, DC: American Association for the Advancement of Science.

Martin, D. (2009). *Elementary science methods: A constructivist approach* (5th ed.). Stamford, CT: Cengage.

McAfee, O., Leong, D., & Bodrova, E. (2004). *Basics of assessment*. Washington, DC: National Association for the Education of Young Children.

Meisels, S., Harrington, H., McMahon, P., Dichtelmiller, M., & Jablon, J. (2001). *Thinking like a teacher: Using observational assessment to improve teaching and learning*. Boston: Allyn and Bacon.

Meisels, S., Marsden, D., Jablon, J., Dorfman, A., & Dichtelmiller, M. (2009). *The work sampling system*. New York: Pearson.

Monighan-Nourot, P., Scales, B., Van Hoorn, J., with Almy, M. (1987). *Looking at children's play: A bridge between theory and practice*. New York: Teachers College Press.

Mulcahey, C. (2009). *The story in the picture: Inquiry and artmaking with young children*. New York: Teachers College Press.

National Association for the Education of Young Children & National Association of Early Childhood Specialists in State Departments of Education. (2002). *Early learning standards: Creating the conditions for success* [Joint Position statement]. Available online at www.naeyc.org/dap

National Board for Professional Teaching Standards. (2000). *Early childhood and middle childhood art standards*. Arlington, VA: Author.

National Council for the Social Studies. (2004). *Curriculum standards for social studies: Expectation of excellence*. Washington, DC: Author.

National Council of Teachers of Mathematics. (2000). *Principles and standards for school mathematics*. Reston, VA: Author.

National Research Council on Teaching and Learning. (1996). *National science education standards for grades K–4*. Washington, DC: National Academy Press.

National Research Council on Teaching and Learning. (2005). *Recommendations for early childhood education: Collaboration for change*. Washington, DC: National Academy Press.

New York City Department of Education. (2003). *Prekindergarten performance standards*. New York: Author.

Ollila, L., & Mayfield, M. (Eds.). (1992). *Emerging literacy: Preschool, kindergarten, and primary grades*. Needham Heights, MA: Allyn and Bacon.

Paley, V. (1981). *Wally's stories: Conversations in the kindergarten*. Cambridge, MA: Harvard University Press.

Paley, V. (2004). *A child's work: The importance of fantasy play*. Chicago: University of Chicago Press.

Paley, V. (2010). *The boy on the beach: Building community through play*. Chicago: University of Chicago Press.

Pelo, A. (2007). *The language of art: Inquiry-based studio practices in early childhood settings*. St. Paul, MN: Redleaf Press.

Pennsylvania Department of Education and Department of Public Welfare. (2009). *Pennsylvania learning standards for early childhood–Revised*. Harrisburg, PA: Author.

Piaget, J. (1977). *The development of thought: Equilibration of cognitive structures.* New York: Viking.

Piaget, J., & Inhelder, B. (1969). *The psychology of the child.* New York: Basic Books.

Read, K. (1971). *The nursery school: A human relationships laboratory* (5th ed.). Philadelphia: Saunders.

Reynolds, G., & Jones, E. (1997). *Master players: Learning from children at play.* New York: Teachers College Press.

Roschelle, J. (1995). Learning in interactive environments: Prior knowledge and new experience. In J. H. Falk & L. D. Dierking (Eds.), *Public institutions for personal learning: Establishing a research agenda* (pp. 37–51). Washington, DC: American Association of Museums.

Ruddell, R., & Ruddell, M. (1995). *Teaching children to read and write: Becoming an influential teacher.* New York: Allyn and Bacon.

Scheinfeld, D. R., Haigh, J. M., & Scheinfeld, S. (2008). *We are all explorers: Learning and teaching with Reggio principles in urban settings.* New York: Teachers College Press.

Schwartz, S. (2005). *Teaching young children mathematics.* Westport, CT: Praeger/Greenwood.

Schickedanz, J. (2008). *Increasing the power of instruction: Integration of language, literacy, and math across the preschool day.* Washington, DC: National Association for the Education of Young Children.

Schirrmacher, R. (1993). *Art and creative development for young children* (2nd ed.). Albany, NY: Delmar.

Seefeldt, C., & Wasik, B. (2006). *Early education: Three-, four- and five-year-olds go to school* (2nd ed.). Upper Saddle River, NJ: Pearson.

Shepard, L., Kagan, S., & Wurtz, E. (1998). *Principles and recommendations for early childhood assessments.* Washington, DC: National Education Goals Panel.

Slavin, R., Madden, N., Dolan, L., & Wasik, B. (1996). *Every child/every school: Success for all.* Thousand Oaks, CA: Corwin.

Smilansky, S. (1968). *The effects of sociodramatic play on disadvantaged preschool children.* New York: John Wiley and Sons.

Sophian, C. (1999). Children's ways of knowing: Lessons from cognitive development research. In J. Copley (Ed.), *Mathematics in the early years* (pp. 11–20). Washington, DC: National Association for the Education of Young Children and National Council for Teachers of Mathematics.

Thompson, G. (1991). *Teaching through themes.* New York: Scholastic.

Thompson, S. K. (2005). *Children as illustrators: Making meaning through art and language.* Washington, DC: National Association for the Education of Young Children.

Van Hoorn, J., Nourot, P., Scales, B., & Alward, K. (1999). *Play at the center of the curriculum* (2nd ed.). Upper Saddle River, NJ: Prentice Hall.

Vygotsky, L. S. (1978). *Mind in society.* Cambridge, MA: Harvard University Press.

Wann, K., Dorn, M., & Liddle, E. (1962). *Fostering intellectual development in young children.* New York: Teachers College Press.

Wick, W. (1997). *A drop of water.* New York: Scholastic Press.

Wien, C. A. (2008). Emergent curriculum. In C. A. Wien (Ed.), *Emergent curriculum in the primary classroom: Interpreting the Reggio Emilia approach in schools* (pp. 5–16). New York: Teachers College Press.

Williams, D. (1995). *Teaching mathematics through children's art.* Portsmouth, NH: Heinemann.

Williams, L., & DeGaetano, Y. (1985). *Alerta: A multicultural, bilingual approach to teaching young children.* Menlo Park, CA: Addison-Wesley.

Williams, R., Rockwell, R., & Sherwood, E. (1987). *Mudpies to magnets: A preschool science curriculum.* Mt. Rainier, MD: Gryphon House.

Worth, K., & Grollman, S. (2003). *Worms, shadows and whirlpools.* Portsmouth, NH: Heinemann.

Wortham, S. (2001). *Assessment in early childhood education* (3rd ed.). Upper Saddle River, NJ: Prentice Hall.

Wortham, S. (2006). *Early childhood curriculum: Developmental bases for learning and teaching* (4th ed.). Upper Saddle River, NJ: Pearson Education.

SOURCES FOR PUBLICATION OF CURRICULUM STANDARDS

International Reading Association (IRA). Newark, DE

National Association for the Education of Young Children (NAEYC). Washington, DC

National Council of Teachers of Mathematics (NCTM). Reston, VA

National Council for the Social Studies (NCSS). Baltimore, MD

National Council for the Teachers of English (NCTE). Urbana, IL

National Science Teachers Association (NSTA). Arlington, VA

United States Department of Education (USDE). Washington, DC

CHILDREN'S BOOKS USED IN SHOE THEME

Bowie, C. (2002). *Big toes, little toes.* Watertown, MA: Charlesbridge.

Burton, M., & Ransome, J. (1994). *My best shoes.* New York: Tambourine Books.

Collins, H. (1997). *One, two, buckle my shoe.* Niagara Falls, NY: Kids Can Press.

Cote, N. (1998). *Flip-flops.* Morton Grove, IL: Whitman.

Cottle, J. (1999). *Emily's shoes.* New York: Grolier.

Daniels, T., & Foster, T. (1999). *The feet in the gym.* Delray Beach, FL: Winslow Press.

De Regniers, B., & Sendak, M. (1997). *What can you do with a shoe?* New York: Aladdin.

Dorros, A. (1982). *Alligator shoes.* New York: Dutton Children's Books.

Garland, S. (1997). *Ellie's shoes.* London: Random House.

Grimes, N., & Widener, T. (Ill.). (2000). *Shoe magic.* New York: Orchard Books.

Grover, M. (1998). *So many kinds of shoes.* New York: Harcourt Brace.

Harper, J., & Osborn, K. (1999). *I forgot my shoes.* New York: Putnam.

Hoban, T. (1986). *Red, blue, yellow shoe.* New York: Greenwillow.

Isadora, R. (2003). *On your toes: A ballet A B C.* New York: Greenwillow.

Lodge, B. (2000). *Shoe shoe baby.* New York: Random House.

Miller, M. (1991). *Whose shoes?* New York: Greenwillow.

Patrick, D. (1993). *Red dancing shoes.* New York: Tambourine Books.

Rollings, S. (2000). *New shoes.* New York: Orchard Books.

Schaefer, C. (1996). *The squiggle.* New York: Crown Publishers.

Schreiber, A. (1998). *Shoes, shoes, shoes.* New York: Scholastic.

Wildsmith, B. (1998). *Whose shoes?* New York: Oxford.

Winthrop, E. (1986). *Shoes.* New York: HarperCollins.

Index

About the Authors

Sydney L. Schwartz is a professor emerita of Queens College of the City University of New York. Her scholarship, focusing on strengthening content in early childhood programs, has spanned a half a century. Dr. Schwartz is the author of many articles, chapters in books, and books dealing with the early childhood curriculum, most recently one on *Teaching Young Children Mathematics*.

Sherry M. Copeland is an experienced early childhood teacher, teacher trainer, advocate, and administrator of early childhood programs. Her career spans 40 years, during which time she has focused her professional energies on improving the quality of education for young children, with a special emphasis on strengthening content in action-based programs. Dr. Copeland has presented at national, state, and local conferences, has been a member of local and statewide policy committees, and has participated in writing early childhood curriculum and learning standards.